Letts

GCSE SUCCESS

VISUAL REVISION GUIDE

GERMAN

Authors

Clive Bell & Lawrence Briggs

CONTENTS

MY WORLD

HOLIDAY TIME AND TRAVEL 1

HOLIDAY TIME AND TRAVEL 2

WORK AND LIFESTYLE

THE YOUNG PERSON IN SOCIETY

UNIVERSAL LANGUAGE

NUMBERS

0	Null
1	eins
2	zwei
3	drei
4	vier
5	fünf
6	sechs
7	sieben
8	acht
9	neun
10	zehn
11	elf
12	zwölf
13	dreizehn
14	vierzehn
15	fünfzehn
16	sechzehn
17	siebzehn
18	achtzehn
19	neunzehn
20	zwanzig
21	einundzwanzig
22	zweiundzwanzig
23	dreiundzwanzig
24	vierundzwanzig
30	dreißig
31	einunddreißig
40	vierzig
50	fünfzig
60	sechzig
70	siebzig
80	achtzig
90	neunzig
100	hundert
101	hunderteins
121	hunderteinundzwanzig
1000	tausend
1000000	eine Million

1ST, 2ND, 3RD...

1st	der Erste/die Erste/das Erste
2nd	der Zweite/die Zweite/das Zweite
3rd	der Dritte/die Dritte/das Dritte
4th	der Vierte/die Vierte/das Vierte
5th	der Fünfte/die Fünfte/das Fünfte, etc.

TIME

Wieviel Uhr ist es?	What time is it?
Wie spät ist es?	What time is it?
Es ist...	It's...
Mittag/Mitternacht	midday/midnight
ein Uhr	one o'clock
zwei Uhr	two o'clock
fünf nach drei	five past three
Viertel nach vier	quarter past four
halb sechs	half past five
zwanzig vor sechs	twenty to six
Viertel vor sieben	quarter to seven

24-HOUR TIMES

It is/at...	Es ist/um...
1.00	ein Uhr
2.15	zwei Uhr fünfzehn
12.00	zwölf Uhr
13.30	dreizehn Uhr dreißig
21.40	einundzwanzig Uhr vierzig
24.00	vierundzwanzig Uhr

BEING POLITE

If you are talking to:

- **one friend or relative (or a pet), use 'du'**
- **an adult, a stranger or more than one person, use 'Sie'**
- **more than one relative or friend, use 'ihr'**

THE ALPHABET

Try this version of the German alphabet:

a	ah	h	hah	r	air
b	bay	i	ee	s	ess
c	tsay	j	yacht	t	tay
d	day	k	ka	u	ooh
e	eh	l	ell	v	fau
f	eff	m	em	w	vay
g	gay	n	en	x	eex
		o	oh	y	oopsilon
		þ	þay	z	zet
		q	koo		

SHORT ANSWERS AND LINK WORDS (CONJUNCTIONS)

Use these for (some) answers in the oral exam and in your written work, especially the link words (conjunctions):

SHORT ANSWERS

(Ja), alles klar	(Yes) agreed/okay/I understand
Sicher/natürlich	Certainly/of course
Ja gerne	Yes, I do/please, all right
Sofort	Straight away
Warte(n) (Sie) mal!	Just (wait) a moment!
Was?/wie bitte?	What?/pardon?
Das stimmt (nicht)	That's (not) true/right
Aber nein!	No, not at all!
Noch nicht	Not yet
Vielleicht	Perhaps
Ich weiß nicht	I don't know

LINK WORDS (CONJUNCTIONS)

und	and
aber	but
sondern	but **(after a negative)**
also	so, therefore
darum	then, therefore
dann	then
danach	afterwards
schließlich/endlich	finally, at last
denn/weil	because
da	as, since (because)
oder	or
sonst	if not, otherwise

DAYS AND MONTHS

Montag	Monday	Januar	January
Dienstag	Tuesday	Februar	February
		März	March
Mittwoch	Wednesday	April	April
		Mai	May
Donnerstag	Thursday	Juni	June
		Juli	July
Freitag	Friday	August	August
		September	September
Samstag	Saturday	Oktober	October
		November	November
Sonntag	Sunday	Dezember	December

Der wievielte ist heute? What's the date today?
Es ist… It's…
… the 2nd of January … der zweite Januar
On the 30th of June Am 30. (dreißigsten) Juni

QUESTIONS

Asking questions can earn lots of marks:
- wann? when?
- was? what?
- wer? who?
- wie…? (Wie spät ist es?) what…? (What time is it?)
- wo? where?
- wohin? where to?
- woher? where from?
- warum? why?
- wie? (Wie schreibt man das?/Wie heißt du?) how…?/what…? (How do you spell that? What is your name?)

Whether you're answering questions at Foundation Level or Higher Level, always follow these rules:

- Stick to the instructions and give the examiners what they are asking for:
  i) A short list, a message and a letter (Foundation)
  ii) A letter and a descriptive or imaginative piece of text (Higher).
- Once you have finished writing, check your answers as if you were marking them. Have you included everything the question has asked you to include?
- Remember, at Foundation Level about 50% of your marks are for communication and the other half are for grammar and quality of language; at Higher Level about 40% of your marks are for communication, so grammar and quality of language are worth about 60%.
- To help you boost your accuracy levels, we have colour coded the lists of nouns in this book: blue for Masculine nouns, red for Feminine nouns, green for Neuter nouns and yellow for Plurals.
- Always show what you know, especially how you can use the tenses, express your opinions and make your emails, letters and descriptions interesting and varied. Check, too, that you have set out formal/business letters (to hotels, campsites, etc.) correctly.
- Use search engines such as www.yahoo.de to access on-line German dictionaries and to get up-to-date information on any subject you like in German.

Here are some examples to guide you, starting with Foundation Level tasks:

1. Your German friend is coming to stay and wants to know what presents to bring for your family. Write a list in German giving four more presents.

Example	Bücher
1	
2	
3	
4	
(2 marks)	

Example answer:

1. Pralinen
2. Parfüm
3. Bonbons
4. Schlüsselring

2. Now you are arranging a barbecue with a German friend, who sends you the following email, asking some questions.

Machen wir eine Grillparty?
Wann denn?
Was kaufen wir dafür ein?
Wo treffen wir uns?
Fährst du mit dem Zug?
Um wieviel Uhr kommst du wieder nach Hause?
Bis bald!
Gruss
Chris

Write a reply, answering Chris's questions in German in full sentences each time.
Example: Ja, ich mache gerne eine Grillparty.

Write:
When the barbecue is (day and time)
Machen wir die Grillparty am Donnerstag um sieben Uhr
What you are buying
Ich kaufe Brot und Bratwürste
Where you are meeting
Treffen wir uns in der Stadtmitte

How you are getting there
Ich nehme den Zug
When you plan to go home
Um halb zehn komme ich wieder nach Hause
(20 marks)

3. Read the letter you have received from your German penfriend, Anna. She wants to know about your plans for the Christmas holidays and about your friends.

Lieber Chris,
Fröhliche Weihnachten! Bald sind die Weihnachtsferien!
Das freut mich sehr denn ich bin eigentlich sehr müde. Und du?
Leider muss ich während der Ferien arbeiten, aber ich gehe sowieso mit meinen Freunden aus.
Gehst du mit deinen Freunden aus? Was habt ihr letztes Wochenende gemacht? Wie sind deine Freunde? Die sind ganz lieb, oder?
Fährst du in Urlaub? Hoffentlich bleibst du nicht zu Hause?
Schreib bald wieder!
Gruss
Anna

Schreib einen Brief auf Deutsch an Anna. Beantworte folgende Fragen:

1. *Bist du auch müde?*
2. *Wann gehst du mit deinen Freunden aus?*
3. *Wo geht ihr hin?*
4. *Und letztes Wochende? Wo seid ihr hingegangen?*
5. *Beschreibe deine Freunde.*
6. *Bleibst du in den Weihnachtsferien zu Hause?*
7. *Stell ihr eine Frage über ihre Ferien und ihre Freunde.*

EXAMPLE:

Liebe Anna,

Fröhliche Weihnachten gleichfalls.   Ich auch bin todmüde – ich habe in der Schule schwer gearbeitet.   Normalerweise gehe ich am Wochende mit meinen Freunden aus.   Sie sind ganz sportlich, darum haben wir letzten Samstag ein Basketballspiel im Sportzentrum gemacht. Das war toll!

Ich gehe in den Ferien zu meinen Großeltern. Das mache ich gerne, weil sie so lieb sind!   Und du? Bleibst du zu Hause oder gehst du auch zu deinen Großeltern?

Bis bald!

Gruss

Chris

• *If the letter is formal, you'll still need to follow the guidance and questions provided, but you should make sure the following elements are included:*

1.	The address of the business to which you are writing	*Campingplatz 'Sonnenecke'* *Dorfstraße* *20813 HOHENRADEN*
2.	Your home town and date	*Southampton, den 22. Mai 2002*
3.	The correct/polite way to talk to the person you are writing to (Sehr geehrter Herr!/Sehr geehrte Dame!)	*Sehr geehrter Herr!* *Haben Sie noch Platz ...*
4.	One of the various ways of signing off correctly	*Hochachtungsvoll* *... (+ your signature)*

Last but not least, if you are asked, as a Higher Level task, to write an imaginative piece of text or to comment on an article, make full use of the prompt questions or text and make sure you work in past, present and future tenses, using plenty of link words and opinions, and even the occasional bit of familiar or slang German you have learned. (See 'Ein Unfall', page 51 and 'Angriff aus Mars', pages 63 and 65, for examples of imaginative texts.)

Alles Gute!

SELF, FAMILY AND FRIENDS ①

QUESTIONS: YOUR VOICE OR YOUR VERB

HOW TO ASK QUESTIONS

1. Intonation: use the sound of your voice
Du hast Haustiere?
You have pets?

2. Switch the pronoun (du) and the verb (hast)
Hast du Haustiere?
Do you have pets?

Ja, ich habe eine Katze
Yes, I have a cat

WWW.
For other questions, just imagine you're on the World Wide Web:

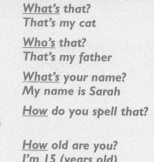

W	*Was ist das?*	*What's that?*
	Das ist meine Katze	*That's my cat*
W	*Wer ist das?*	*Who's that?*
	Das ist mein Vater	*That's my father*
W	*Wie heißt du?*	*What's your name?*
	Ich heiße Sarah	*My name is Sarah*
W	*Wie schreibt man das?*	*How do you spell that?*
	S(ess) – A(ah) – R(air) – A(ah) – H(hah)	
W	*Wie alt bist du?*	*How old are you?*
	Ich bin fünfzehn (Jahre alt)	*I'm 15 (years old)*
W	*Wann hast du Geburtstag?*	*When's your birthday?*
	Am 30. (dreißigsten) Mai	*30th May*
W	*Wo wohnst du?*	*Where do you live?*
	Ich wohne in Manchester	*I live in Manchester*
W	*Warum?*	*Why?*
	Warum denn nicht?! Es ist eine schöne Stadt	*Why not?! It's a nice town*

VITAL VERBS

Exchange all the personal information you need with these key verbs:

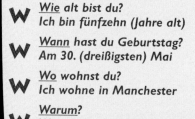

1 *Heißen (to be called)*

Ich heiße	My name is ...	**Alex**
Du heißt	Your name is ...	**Chris**
Er heißt	His name is ...	**Martin**
Sie heißt	Her name is ...	**Martina**

2 *Haben (to have)*

Ich habe keine Geschwister	I have no brothes orsisters
Du hast blaue Augen	You have blue eyes
Er hat kurzes Haar	He has short hair
Sie hat einen Bruder und eine Halbschwester	She has a brother and a step-sister

3 *Sein (to be)*

Ich bin fünfzehn	I am 15
Du bist fleißig	You are hard-working
Er ist groß und schlank	He is tall and slim
Sie ist sehr sportlich	She is very sporty

OCCUPATIONS

Ärzt/Ärztin	doctor
Bäcker/-in	baker
Briefträger/-in	postman/woman
Kassierer/-in	cashier, checkout person
Kaufmann	sales rep (male)
Kauffrau	sales rep (female)
Kellner/-in	waiter/waitress
Krankenpfleger	nurse (male)
Krankenschwester	nurse (female)
Lehrer/-in	teacher
Mechaniker/-in	mechanic
Polizist/-in	policeman/woman
Sekretär/-in	secretary
Steward/-ess	steward/air hostess
Verkäufer/-in	shop assistant
Zahnarzt/-ärztin	dentist
arbeitslos	unemployed

ADJECTIVES

doof/dumm	daft/stupid	hübsch	pretty
ehrlich	honest	humorlos	no sense of humour
faul	lazy		
fleißig	hard-working	klein	small
frech	rude	langweilig	boring
freundlich	friendly	launisch	moody
geschwätzig	talkative	nett	nice
groß	tall	schüchtern	shy
hässlich	ugly	sportlich	sporty
hilfsbereit	helpful	süß	sweet
(un)höflich	(im)polite	witzig	funny, witty

MARRIAGE, ETC

geschieden	divorced
getrennt	separated
ledig	single
Frau	woman, wife
Mann	man, husband
Schwager	brother-in-law
Schwägerin	sister-in-law
Schwiegermutter	mother-in-law
Schwiegervater	father-in-law
verheiratet	married

NATIONALITIES

Ich bin ...	I am ...
Er/sie ist ...	He/she is ...

Amerikaner/-in	American	Österreicher/-in	Austrian
Belgier/-in	Belgian	Schotte/-in	Scottish
Brite/Britin	British	Schweizer/-in	Swiss
Deutscher/Deutsche	German	Spanier/-in	Spanish
Engländer/-in	English	Türke/-in	Turkish
Franzose/Französin	French	Waliser/-in	Welsh
Griecher/-in	Greek		
Holländer/-in	Dutch		
Ire/Irin	Irish		
Italiener/-in	Italian		

Note
kommen aus = to come from
Mein Vater kommt aus Luxemburg = My father comes from Luxembourg

INTRODUCING FAMILY, FRIENDS & PETS

Das ist mein/-e ...	That's my ...
Brieffreund/-in	penfriend
Vater	father
Mutter	mother
Großvater	grandfather
Großmutter	grandmother
Bruder	brother
Schwester	sister
Halbbruder	half-/step-brother
Halbschwester	half-/step-sister
Onkel	uncle
Tante	aunt
Cousin/Vetter	cousin
Kusine	cousin
Hamster	hamster
Maus	mouse
Hund	dog
Katze	cat
Wellensittich	budgie
Schildkröte	tortoise

Remember the neuter nouns for pets and the plurals:

Das sind meine ...	These are my ...
mein Kaninchen	my rabbit
Eltern	parents
mein Meerschweinchen	my guinea pig
Großeltern	grandparents
mein Pferd	my horse
Fische	fish

SUBJECT PRONOUNS

These tell you who does what

ich	I
du/Sie	you
er	he
sie	she
es	it
man	we, you, people, one
wir	we
Sie	you
ihr	you (plural of 'du')
sie	they

There are three words for 'you': use 'du' with one person you know well. Use 'ihr' with more than one person you know well. use 'Sie' for one or more than one person you know less well or who is older than you/an adult.

'Man' is used a lot instead of 'wir' to say 'we', or 'you' in sentences such as: 'How do you spell that?' (Wie schreibt man das?) or 'When do we arrive?'(Wann kommt man an?).

ICH, DU UND DIE ELTERN

Hallo! Ich heiße Nadia. Ich bin fünfzehn Jahre alt und ich wohne in Southampton in Südengland. Und du?
Hello. My name's Nadia. I'm 15 years old and I live in Southampton in the south of England. What about you?

Ich heiße Thomas und ich bin sechzehn Jahre alt. Ich wohne in West Bromwich in Mittelengland. Bist du Deutsche?
My name's Thomas and I'm 16 years old. I live in West Bromwich in the Midlands. Are you German?

Ja, mein Vater ist Deutscher. Er kommt aus Hamburg, aber meine Mutter ist Engländerin.
Yes, my father is German. He comes from Hamburg, but my mother is English.

Was macht dein Vater? Ist er Lehrer oder was?
What does your father do? Is he a teacher or something?

Ach nein, der ist kein Lehrer. Er ist Kaufmann bei einer englischen Firma. Meine Mutter ist aber Grundschullehrerin. Und deine Eltern?
Oh no, he's not a teacher. He's a sales rep for an English company. But my mother is a primary school teacher. What about your parents?

Examiner's Top Tip
Remember the expression 'gut aus-kommen mit' (to get on well with), if you want to boost your marks, eg Ich komme mit seiner Frau nicht gut aus. I don't get on well with his wife.

Sie sind geschieden. Ich wohne mit meiner Mutter. Mein Vater ist wieder verheiratet aber ich finde seine Frau ganz blöd.
They are divorced. My father has remarried, but I think his wife is really stupid.

SELF, FAMILY AND FRIENDS ②

GESCHWISTER UND TIERE

Hast du Geschwister?
Do you have brothers or sisters?

Ja, ich habe eine ältere Schwester und einen Halbbruder, aber ich kenne ihn nicht gut. Meine Schwester heißt Nicky.
Yes, I have an elder sister and a stepbrother, but I don't know him very well. My sister's name is Nicky

Kommst du mit ihr gut aus?
Do you get on well with her?

Ja, sicher, ich finde sie toll. Sie hat jede Menge Freunde und sie ist sehr clever und sehr witzig.
Yes, sure, I think she's great. She's got loads of friends and she's very clever and very funny.

Wie sieht sie aus?
What does she look like?

Sie ist mittelgroß und schlank. Sie hat lange schwarze Haare und graue Augen. Sie trägt auch eine Brille. Was noch? Ach ja, sie ist sehr sportlich und spielt besonders gern Fußball. Treibst du auch gern Sport?
She's of average height and slim. She has long black hair and grey eyes. She also wears glasses. What else? Oh yes, she's very sporty and particularly likes playing football. Do you like doing sport?

Nein, aber ich gehe gern mit meinem Hund spazieren. Hast du Haustiere?
No, but I like taking my dog for walks. Have you got any pets?

Wir haben eine schwarze Katze namens Mitzi, aber ich finde sie launisch und langweilig. Sie schläft den ganzen Tag lang!
We have a black cat called Mitzi, but I find her moody and boring. She sleeps all day long!

Bist du doof! Alle Katzen schlafen so lange!
Don't be so daft! All cats sleep that long!

Examiner's Top Tip
Use these sections to write emails, faxes and short letters to German friends, or in exams.

QUICK TEST

Say/write it in English:
1. Ich heiße Stefan.
2. Hast du Haustiere?
3. Wann hast du Geburtstag?
4. Wie ist deine Adresse?

Say/write it in German:
5. What's your name?
6. How old are you?
7. I'm very shy.
8. She's got green eyes.
9. Does he like reading?
10. Here's my brother. He's very lazy but very funny.

1. My name's Stefan.
2. Have you got any pets?
3. When is your birthday?
4. What's your address?
5. Wie heißt du?
6. Wie alt bist du?
7. Ich bin sehr schüchtern.
8. Sie hat grüne Augen.
9. Liest er gern?
10. Das ist mein Bruder. Er ist sehr faul aber (auch) sehr witzig.

INTERESTS AND HOBBIES

INFINITIVES

WHAT ARE INFINITIVES? WHY ARE THEY IMPORTANT? WHAT ARE THEY IN ENGLISH? HOW MANY ARE THERE?

- *Infinitives are the key to all verbs.*
- *They are the starting point for all tenses. Look at the opposite page and see how they help to form the present tense*
- *In English they translate as 'to …', e.g. gehen = to go, machen = to do.*
- *Although there are thousands of them, they all end in -n and most of them end in -en, e.g. spielen = to play, schwimmen = to swim (but sein = to be).*
- *Some end in -eln, e.g. segeln = to sail.*
- *A few others end in -ern, e.g. rudern = to row (a boat)*

Examiner's Top Tip
Remember that there are several ways of saying 'you' in German, depending on whether you are talking to one or more people and on how well you know them. Look again at the Subject Pronouns box on page 9, if you're still not sure.

MODAL VERBS

When you talk about things you want to do, can/are able to do, must/have to do, are supposed to do or are allowed to do, you are using modal verbs. These are almost always followed by an infinitive:

können	to be able (to)
ich kann	I can (am able to)
du kannst	you can (are able to)
er/sie/es kann	he/she/it can (is able to)
man kann	one/we/you/they can (are able to)
wir können	we can (are able to)
ihr könnt	you can (are able to)
Sie können	you can (are able to)
sie können	they can (are able to)

wollen	to want (to)
ich will	I want
du willst	you want
er/sie/es will	he/she/it wants
man will	one/we/you/they want
wir wollen	we want
ihr wollt	you want
Sie wollen	you want
sie wollen	they want

dürfen	to be allowed to
ich darf	I am allowed to
du darfst	you are allowed to
er/sie/es darf	he/she/it is allowed to
man darf	one/we/you/they is/are allowed to
wir dürfen	we are allowed to
ihr dürft	you are allowed to
Sie dürfen	you are allowed to
sie dürfen	they are allowed to

müssen	must/to have to
ich muss	I must (have to)
du musst	you must (have to)
er/sie/es muss	he/she/it must (has to)
man muss	one/we/you/they must (have/has to)
wir müssen	we must (have to)
ihr müsst	you must (have to)
Sie müssen	you must (have to)
sie müssen	they must (have to)

sollen	to be supposed to
ich soll	I am supposed to
du sollst	you are supposed to
er/sie/es soll	he/she/it is supposed to
man soll	one/we/you/they is/are supposed to
wir sollen	we are supposed to
ihr sollt	you are supposed to
Sie sollen	you are supposed to
sie sollen	they are supposed to

Darf ich fernsehen? — **Am I allowed to watch TV?**
Du musst gewinnen — **You must win**
Sie kann gut skifahren — **She can ski well**
Wir sollen lesen — **We are supposed to read**
Wollt ihr trainieren? — **Do you want to train?**

REGULAR VERBS

Most verbs in German are regular (or 'weak' because they follow the same pattern). To form the present tense of regular verbs, remove the ending of the infinitive (-en or -n) and put on the following endings:

spiel<u>en</u>	to play
ich spiele	I play/am playing
du spielst	you play/are playing
er/sie/es spielt	he/she/it plays/is playing
man spielt	one/we/you/they/people plays(s)/is/are playing
wir spielen	we play/are playing
ihr spielt	you play/are playing
Sie spielen	you play/are playing
sie spielen	they play/are playing

angel<u>n</u>	to fish
ich angele	I fish/am fishing
du angelst	you fish/are fishing
er/sie/es angelt	the/she/it fishes/is fishing
man angelt	one/we/you/they/people fish(es)/ is/are fishing
wir angeln	we fish/are fishing
ihr angelt	you fish/are fishing
Sie angeln	you fish/are fishing
sie angeln	they fish/are fishing

ruder<u>n</u>	to row, steer
ich rudere	I row/am rowing
du ruderst	you row/are rowing
er/sie/es rudert	he/she/it rows/is rowing
man rudert	one/we/you/they/people row(s)/is/are rowing
wir rudern	we row/are rowing
ihr rudert	you row/are rowing
Sie rudern	you row/are rowing
sie rudern	they row/are rowing

IRREGULAR VERBS

Many of the irregular verbs(also called 'strong' or 'mixed' verbs, because they change in different ways and in different tenses) are not a problem in the present tense, because they look like weak verbs. For example, schwimmen ('to swim'), gehen ('to go'), kommen ('to come'), reiten ('to ride'), singen ('to sing') and (Sport) treiben ('to do sport'), are all irregular verbs but they have the same endings as weak verbs in the present tense:

Ich schwimme gern	I like swimming
Gehst du spazieren?	Are you going for a walk?
Sie reitet oft Pferd	She often goes horse riding
Ihr singt so schön	You sing so beautifully
Abends treiben sie Sport	They do sport in the evenings

However, there are several verbs that change differently in the present tense. You can hear the changes as well as see them, in the second and third person singular forms:

skifahren	to ski (where the <u>a</u> changes to <u>ä</u>)
ich fahre ski	I go skiing
du f<u>ä</u>hrst ski	you go skiing
er/sie/es f<u>ä</u>hrt ski	he/she/it goes skiing
wir fahren ski	we go skiing
ihr fahrt ski	you go skiing
Sie fahren ski	you go skiing
sie fahren ski	they go skiing

Two other verbs that follow this irregular pattern are:
- <u>schlafen</u> ('to sleep') → (du schl<u>ä</u>fst) ('you sleep'), er schl<u>ä</u>ft ('he sleeps')
- laufen ('to go/run') → (du l<u>ä</u>ufst (Rollschuh) ('you go (rollerskating)'), sie l<u>ä</u>uft (Rollschuh) ('she goes (rollerskating)')

treffen	to meet (where the <u>e</u> changes to <u>i</u>)
ich treffe	I am meeting
du tr<u>i</u>ffst	you are meeting
er/sie/es tr<u>i</u>fft	he/she/it is meeting
wir treffen	we are meeting
ihr trefft	you are meeting
Sie treffen	you are meeting
sie treffen	they are meeting

Two other verbs that follow this irregular pattern are:
- <u>helfen</u> ('to help') → (du h<u>i</u>lfst ('you are helping'), er h<u>i</u>lft ('he is helping')
- <u>nehmen</u> ('to take') → (du n<u>i</u>mmst ('you take'), sie n<u>i</u>mmt ('she takes')

Examiner's Top Tip
You can use the present tense of 'gehen' (to go) + gern + infinitive, to say you like going to do something:
Ich gehe gern kegeln
I like to go bowling
Gehst du gern tanzen?
Do you like to go dancing?

SPORTS AND HOBBIES

spielen	to play
sammeln	to collect
(an)hören	to listen to
machen	to make, do, (take e.g. photos)

ins Kino gehen	to go to the cinema
Rad fahren	to go cycling
Schlittschun laufen	to go ice skating
Wasserski laufen	to water ski

Masculine (der):

Basketball	basketball
Fußball	football
Handball	handball
Volleyball	volleyball

Feminine (die):

Briefmarke(n)	stamp(s)
Flöte	flute
Gitarre	guitar
Gymnastik	gymnastics
Leichtathletik	athletics
Musik	music

Neuter (das):

Badminton	badminton
Foto(s)	photo(s)
Hockey	hockey
Instrument	instrument
Klavier	piano
Tennis	tennis
Tischtennis	table tennis

FREIZEIT

Was machst du in der Freizeit?
What do you do in your free time?

Das ist verschieden. Bei schönem Wetter gehe ich mit meinen Freunden aus. Wir treiben vielleicht Sport oder gehen spazieren. Wenn* es aber regnet, bleibe ich lieber zu Hause.
That depends. If the weather's fine I go out with my friends. We do some sport or go for a walk. But if it's raining, I prefer to stay at home.

Ach so, du bist Sportler(in)? Was für Sportarten treibst du denn?
So you're a sportsman(woman)? What sports do you do?

Jede Menge. Ich spiele Basketball und Hockey und gehe oft zum Fitnesszentrum.
Loads. I play basketball and hockey and I often go to the fitness centre.

Im Sommer gehe ich gern surfen oder Wasserski laufen. Das macht Spaß.
In the summer I like to go surfing or water skiing. It's good fun.

Was machst du sonst, zu Hause zum Beispiel?
What do you do apart from that, for example when you're at home?

Tja ... ich ruhe mich aus, ich spiele mit dem Computer, rufe meine Freunde an, alles was.
Well ... I relax, play on the computer, phone my friends, that sort of thing.

Examiner's Top Tip
*Wenn ... If
Remember that 'Wenn' changes the word order by sending the verb to the end of its clause

NACH DER SCHULE

Was machen wir nach der Schule?
What are we doing after school?

Nichts. Ich muss meine Hausaufgaben machen. Hast du doch keine?
Nothing. I have to do my homework. Haven't you got any?

Doch, ich will sie aber nicht machen.
Yes, I have, but I don't want to do it.

Was willst du denn machen? Wir können vielleicht später ausgehen?
What do you want to do then? Perhaps we can go out later?
Ich darf nicht. Wir müssen nämlich meine Großeltern besuchen. Die sind ganz lieb aber....
I'm not allowed to. We have to go and visit my grandparents. They're really nice but....

Ach schade! Kannst du am Freitagabend ausgehen? Zum Konzert? Wir können uns um halb neun am Stadion treffen.
That's a shame! Can you come out on Friday evening? To the concert? We can meet up at 8.30 outside the stadium.

Vielleicht. Kannst du mich am Freitagnachmittag anrufen?
Maybe. Can you phone me on Friday afternoon?

AM WOCHENENDE

He du, es ist wieder Freitag. Wir gehen alle heute Abend zum Konzert. Kannst du mitkommen?
Hey you there, it's Friday again. We're all going to the concert tonight. Can you come?

Leider nicht. Meine Eltern sind heute Abend nicht da, darum muss ich mit meiner kleinen Schwester zu Hause bleiben.
Afraid not. My parents aren't in tonight, so I've got to stay at home with my little sister.

Na gut. Fährst du morgen vormittag in die Stadt?
Oh well. Are you going into town tomorrow morning?

Ja, wollen wir uns gegen zehn Uhr im Stadtzentrum treffen?
Yes, shall we meet at about 10 o'clock in the town centre?

Alles klar. Was willst du machen? Eis essen? Ins Kino gehen?
Okay. What do you want to do? Go for an ice cream? Go to the cinema?

Ich will mir einen neuen CD-Spieler kaufen. Gehen wir lieber zum Einkaufszentrum.**
I want to buy a new CD player. Let's go to the shopping centre.

Toll. Bis dann. Tschüss!
Great! See you then. Bye!

INTERESTS AND HOBBIES ②

QUICK TEST

Say/write it in English:

1. Ich muss hier bleiben.

2. Kannst du mitkommen?

3. Was soll man machen?

4. Spielen wir Tischtennis.

Say/write it in German:

5. If it's cold and stormy.

6. What sports do you do?

7. Do you have to do your homework?

8. Are we allowed to play the piano?

9. If I'm at home, I prefer playing on the computer.

10. Do you want to go cycling or ice skating?

Examiner's Top Tip
**Notice how you say 'Let's do …'; simply switch the verb and the subject. This works with lots of verbs:
• Essen wir ein Eis
Let's eat an ice cream
• Treffen wir uns in der Stadt
Let's meet in town

[Answers]
1. I have to stay here.
2. Can you come along/with me (us)?
3. What are you/is one supposed to do?
4. Let's play table tennis.
5. Wenn es kalt und stürmisch ist.
6. Was für Sportarten treibst du?
7. Musst du deine Hausaufgaben machen?
8. Darf man/Dürfen wir Klavier spielen?
9. Wenn ich zu Hause bin, spiele ich lieber mit dem Computer.
10. Willst du Rad fahren oder Schlittschuh laufen?

FASCINATING CASES

NOMINATIVE AND ACCUSATIVE

- Most sentences have a <u>subject</u> and an <u>object</u>.
- The <u>subject</u> = the person or thing doing the action (NB. actions include 'having', 'being', etc., as well as things like 'eating', 'seeing' and 'watching').
- The <u>object</u> = the person or thing having the action done to it/them.
- In German sentences, the <u>subject</u> is in the <u>nominative</u> case and the <u>object</u> is in the <u>accusative</u> case.

Look at these two sentences:
1. Meine Familie hat ein kleines Haus.
2. Mein kleines Haus hat einen Garten, eine Küche und ein Badezimmer.

In the first sentence, the <u>subject</u> (nominative case) is Meine Familie ('doing' the having) and the <u>object</u> (accusative case) is ein kleines Haus.

In the second sentence, though, the house is the <u>subject</u> (nominative) and the garden, kitchen and bathroom are the <u>object</u> (accusative).

The endings on articles and adjectives change, depending on:
- what case they are in.
- the gender of the noun.

The good news is that it's only with masculine nouns that the endings change from nominative to accusative. With feminine, neuter and plural nouns, the endings are the same in both cases. Here is a summary of the endings:

	Masculine	Adjective ending	Feminine	Adjective ending	Neuter	Adjective ending	Plural	Adjective ending
Nominative	der ein/kein/ mein	-e -er	die eine/keine/ meine	-e	das ein/kein/ mein	-e	die eine/keine/ meine	-en
Accusative	den einen/keinen meinen	-en	eine/ keine/ meine	-e	ein/ kein/ mein	-es	keine/ meine	-en

DATIVE

The dative case is used:
- after certain prepositions (see below).
- for the indirect object of a verb (e.g. giving something to someone): Ich gebe <u>meinem</u> Vater ein Geschenk ('I give my father a present'/'I give a present to my father').
- after certain verbs, e.g. helfen ('to help'): Er hilft <u>meiner</u> Mutter ('He's helping/he helps my mother'), gefallen

('to please'): Mein Schalfzimmer gefällt mir gut ('My bedroom pleases me'/'I like my bedroom').

The endings in the dative case are listed below (NB. adjective endings in the dative are easy – always -en, so concentrate on learning the <u>articles</u> and how they change).

	Masculine	Adjective ending	Feminine	Adjective ending	Neuter	Adjective ending	Plural	Adjective ending
Dative	dem einem/ keinem/ meinem	- en	der einer/ keiner/ meiner	-en	das einem/ keinem/ meinem	-en	den keinen/ meinen*	-en

You add an 'n' to most plural nouns in the dative, e.g. Mein Haus hat sieben <u>Zimmer</u>, but Ich wohne in einem Haus mit sieben <u>Zimmern</u>.

PREPOSITIONS AND THE DATIVE

- Some prepositions are <u>always</u> followed by the dative:

aus	out of
*bei	at someone's house; with
gegenüber	opposite
mit	with; 'by' when talking about means of transport
nach	after
seit	since
*von	from, of
*zu	to

- Some prepositions can be followed by either the accusative, or the dative. If no movement is involved, use the dative:

*an	to, at, on
auf	on
hinter	behind
*in	in
neben	next to
über	over, above
unter	under, below
vor	in front of
zwischen	between

You will often need to use prepositions with the dative to describe your home or bedroom:
- Ich wohne <u>in</u> einem alten Haus, <u>mit</u> meiner Mutter und meinen zwei Brüdern.
I live in an old house, with my mother and my two brothers.

- In meinem Schlafzimmer gibt es viele Posters <u>an den</u> Wänden. Mein Computer steht <u>auf</u> einem kleinen Tisch <u>in</u> der Ecke.
In my bedroom, there are lots of posters on the walls. My computer stands on a little table, in the corner.

*These prepositions merge with the definite article in the dative, to create a single word:
bei + dem = beim
von + dem = vom
zu + dem = zum

zu + der = zur
an + dem = am
in + dem = im
e.g. Wir haben sieben Zimmer <u>im</u> Haus. ('We have seven rooms in the house.')

MY HOME ①

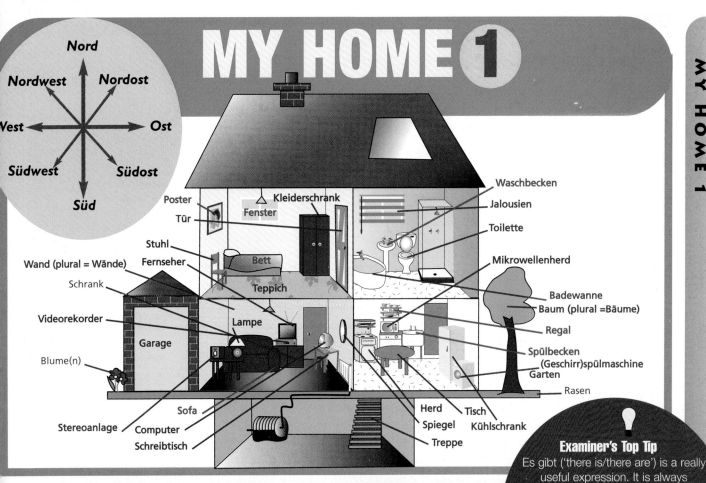

WHERE DO YOU LIVE?

GROßBRITANNIEN

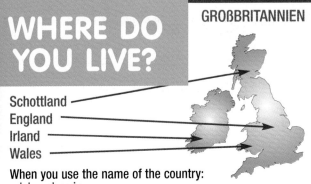

Schottland
England
Irland
Wales

When you use the name of the country:
- Ich wohne <u>in</u> ...
  ('I live in ...')
- Ich komme <u>aus</u> ...
  ('I come from ...')

} Schottland/
Südwestengland (etc.)

But when you want to say just 'the north', 'the east', etc., use the dative:
- Ich wohne <u>im</u> ...
  ('I live in the ...')
- Ich komme <u>aus dem</u> ... ('I come from the ...')

} Norden/Osten

am Stadtrand	on the outskirts in the suburbs
in einer Stadt	in a town
in der Stadtmitte	in the town centre
in einem Dorf	in a village
auf dem Land	in the country(side)
am Meer	by the sea/at the seaside

(ganz) in der Nähe von (+ dative)	(very) near to
(nicht) weit von (+ dative)	(not) far from
vor (+ dative)	in front of
hinter (+ dative)	behind
neben (+ dative)	next to
gegenüber (+ dative)	opposite

For example:
Mein Haus liegt	My house is situated
in der Nähe vom Park	near the park
hinter der Post	behind the post office
gegenüber dem Rathaus	opposite the town hall

Examiner's Top Tip
Es gibt ('there is/there are') is a really useful expression. It is always followed by the accusative case: Was gibt es in deinem Schlafzimmer? ('What is there in your bedroom?') Es gibt einen kleinen Schreibtisch, eine blaue Lampe, viele Posters – und mein Bett, natürlich! ('There's a small desk, a blue lamp, lots of posters – and my bed, of course!')

ADJECTIVES

klein	small
groß	big
alt	old
neu	new
hübsch/nett	pretty
schön	beautiful
hässlich	ugly
bequem	comfortable
still/ruhig	quiet, peaceful
modern	modern

blau	blue
braun	brown
gelb	yellow
grau	grey
grün	green
orange	orange
rosa	pink
rot	red
schwarz	black
weiß	white
violett	purple

dunkel	dark
(dunkelblau	dark blue)
hell	light
(hellgrün	light green)
gestreift	striped
(rot gestreift	with red stripes)
sehr/ganz	very
nicht sehr	not very
ziemlich	quite
ein bisschen	a little bit
zu (klein)	too (small)

MEINE STADT

Wo wohnst du? Where do you live?
Ich wohne seit fünf Jahren in Bristol ... I've lived in Bristol for five years ...
... aber ich komme aus dem Norden und bin in Leeds geboren ... but I come from the north and was born in Leeds.
Bristol ist eine große Stadt in Südwestengland Bristol is a big town in south-west England.
Wohnst du gern hier? Do you like living here?
Bristol gefällt mir gut – es gibt hier viel zu tun – aber ich bin ein Fan von Leeds United. In Leeds konnte ich mir oft die Fußballspiele zuschauen und das fehlt mir sehr. I like Bristol – there's lots to do here – but I'm a Leeds United supporter. In Leeds, I could often go and watch the matches and I miss that a lot.

Examiner's Top Tip
Make sure you give plenty of opinions and back them up with reasons. You can use either weil or denn to mean 'because', but note that when you use weil the verb that follows must go to the end of the sentence.

Wohnst du auf dem Land oder in der Stadt? Do you live in the countryside or in town?
Ich wohne am Stadtrand, etwa acht Kilometer von der Stadtmitte. I live on the outskirts, about eight kilometres from the city centre.
Wir wohnen neben der Kirche und es gibt einige kleinen Geschäfte in der Nähe. We live next to the church and there are some small shops nearby.
Wie fährst du in die Stadt? Und zur Schule? How do you travel into town? And to school?
Meistens fahre ich mit dem Bus in die Stadt, aber ich gehe immer zu Fuß zur Schule. Mostly I travel by bus into town, but I always go to school on foot.

MY HOME ②

BEI MIR ZU HAUSE

Examiner's Top Tip
Notice how you use the present tense with 'seit' to say how long you have been doing something, even though we use the past tense in English. Notice also the word order with 'seit', the time always goes before the place (see page 34);

NB. 'seit' is always followed by the dative (see page 16).

Wohnst du in einem Haus oder in einer Wohnung?
Do you live in a house or a flat?

Ich wohne in einem Haus.
I live in a house.

Wie ist es? Kannst du es beschreiben?
What's it like? Can you describe it?

Es ist ein ziemlich großes, altes Haus, mit sieben Zimmern.
It's quite a big, old house, with seven rooms.

Im Erdgeschoss gibt es die Küche, das Wohnzimmer....
On the ground floor is the kitchen, the living room....

Im ersten Stock haben wir drei Schlafzimmer und ein Badezimmer.
On the first floor we have three bedrooms and a bathroom.

Gefällt dir dein Haus? Warum (nicht)?
Do you like your house? Why (not)?

Nein, es gefällt mir nicht, weil es zu klein ist.
No, I don't like it, because it's too small.

Ja, es gefällt mir sehr, denn es ist bequem und ganz schön.
Yes, I like it a lot, because it's comfortable and quite beautiful.

Examiner's Top Tip
Learn how to ask questions, not just answer them – you'll be expected to ask questions in letters and conversations.

Examiner's Top Tip
Remember: use fahren for 'to go' when referring to travelling by some form of transport, but gehen when referring travelling by foot.

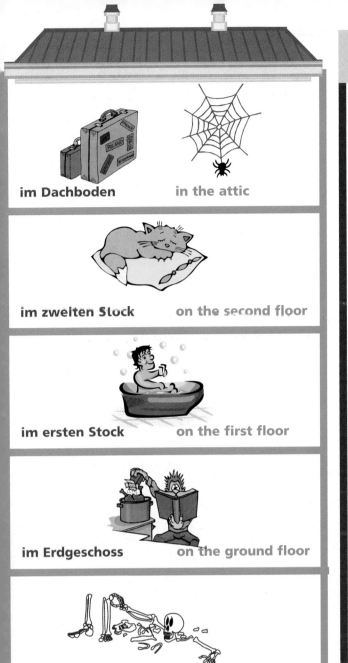

im Dachboden	in the attic
im zweiten Stock	on the second floor
im ersten Stock	on the first floor
im Erdgeschoss	on the ground floor
im Untergeschoss	in the basement

MEIN SCHLAFZIMMER

- **Kannst du mir dein Schlafzimmer beschreiben?**
Can you describe your bedroom?

- **Zum Glück habe ich mein eigenes Schlafzimmer.**
Luckily, I've got my own bedroom.

- **Leider teile ich mein Schlafzimmer mit meinem Bruder.**
Unfortunately, I share a bedroom with my brother.

- **Mein Schlafzimmer ist ziemlich groß.**
My bedroom is quite big.

- **Der Teppich ist rot, die Wände sind weiß und die Vorhänge sind dunkelblau.**
The carpet is red, the walls are white and the curtains are dark blue.

- **In meinem Schalfzimmer gibt es ein Bett, natürlich, einen Kleiderschrank....**
In my bedroom, there's a bed, of course, a wardrobe....

- **Ich mache meine Hausaufgaben in meinem Schlafzimmer, oder ich höre Musik an.**
I do my homework in my bedroom, or I listen to music.

- **Mein Schlafzimmer gefällt mir gut, weil es bequem und ruhig ist.**
I like my bedroom, because it's comfortable and quiet.

Examiner's Top Tip

Try using expressions like 'zum Glück' ('luckily') and 'leider' ('unfortunately') to liven up your speaking and writing. When you use them, watch out for word order! The verb must always be the next word after these expressions and the pronoun comes after the verb, e.g. Leider habe ich keinen Computer ('Unfortunately, I don't have a computer').

QUICK TEST

Say/write it in English:

1. Ich wohne auf dem Land.

2. Wir wohnen seit zehn Jahren in München.

3. Im Erdgeschoss gibt es das Wohnzimmer.

4. Die Vorhänge sind gelb.

Say it/write it in German:

5. It's a small town in north-east England.

6. My house has six rooms.

7. What's your flat like?

8. The carpet is dark red.

9. In my bedroom, there's a computer and lots of posters.

10. I like my bedroom because it's quite big.:

10. Mein Schlafzimmer gefällt mir gut, weil es ziemlich groß ist (or: denn es ist ziemlich groß).
9. In meinem Schlafzimmer gibt es einen Computer und viele Posters.
8. Der Teppich ist dunkelrot.
7. Wie ist deine Wohnung?
6. Mein Haus hat sechs Zimmer.
5. Das ist eine kleine Stadt in Nordostengland.
4. The curtains are yellow.
3. On the ground floor, there's the living-room.
2. We've lived/been living in Munich for 10 years.
1. I live in the countryside.

DAILY ROUTINE (1)

SEPARABLE VERBS

In English there are many verbs that have more than one part, e.g. 'to wake up', 'I wake up early'.

In German, the extra part in verbs like these, called separable verbs, joins on to the front of the infinitive, e.g. aufwachen ('to wake up')

In sentences and clauses (a section of a sentence that has its own verb), the extra part, called a separable prefix, separates and goes straight to the end, e.g. Ich wache immer früh auf ('I always wake up early').

Here are the most common prefixes you'll come across:

ab-
an-
auf-
aus-
ein-
mit-

Look some <u>up</u>, think it <u>through</u>, try them <u>out</u>!

abholen (to pick up)
Wir <u>holen</u> dich morgen <u>ab</u>
We'll pick you up tomorrow
ankommen (to arrive, turn up)
Normalerweise <u>kommt</u> sie spät <u>an</u>
She usually arrives (turns up) late

aufstehen (to get up)
Er steht um sieben Uhr <u>auf</u>
He gets up at seven o'clock

ausgehen (to go out)
Am Wochenende <u>gehen</u>
meine Freunde <u>aus</u>
At the weekend my
friends go out

einladen (to invite)
Oft <u>laden</u> uns meine
Großeltern zum
Mittagessen <u>ein</u>
My grandparents often
invite us to lunch

mitkommen (to come
along with)
Ich gehe in die
Stadt. <u>Kommst</u> du
<u>mit</u>?
I'm going into
town. Are you
coming with
me?

Examiner's Top Tip
Using separable verbs correct[ly]
shows you understand Germa[n]
word order and gains you ex[tra]
credit. Try to find/think of so[me]
other separable verbs tha[t]
have these prefixes:
ein-, durch-, fern-,
-um, -vor,-zu.

Examiner's Top Tip
Reflexive verbs are listed like other ver[bs]
in the dictionary in the infinitive, using [the]
reflexive pronoun sich (oneself):

sich sonnen — to sun oneself
sich ärgern — to get angr[y]
sich ausruhen — to rest, rela[x]
sich beeilen — to hurry (oneself) u[p]
sich langweilen — to feel bore[d]
sich setzen to sit down (seat onese[lf])

REFLEXIVE VERBS

Reflexive verbs are so called because the subject (the person or thing that does the action, e.g. 'washing') is also the direct object (the person or thing that has the action done to them).

Ich amüsiere mich
I'm enjoying myself

Erstens wasche ich den Wagen
First I wash the car ...

... dann wasche ich mich!
... then I wash myself!

Apart from these extra pronouns (ich mich, du dich, er sich, etc.), reflexive verbs follow the same rules as other verbs.

ich wasche mich — I wash (myself)
du wäscht dich — you wash (yourself)
er wäscht sich — he washes (himself)
sie wäscht sich — she washes (herself)
man wäscht sich — one/we/you wash(es) (oneself, ourselves, yourself)
wir waschen uns — we wash (ourselves)
ihr wascht euch — you wash (your selves)
Sie waschen sich — you wash (your self/yourselves)
sie waschen sich — they wash (themselves)

SEPARABLE REFLEXIVE VERBS

There are a few verbs that combine both of the features listed above: reflexive and separable. Just work them through logically:

sich anziehen (to get dressed)
Samstags ziehe ich mich ganz spät an
'On Saturdays I get dressed quite late'

sich ausziehen (to get undressed)
Ziehen Sie sich im Umkleideraum aus
'Get undressed in the changing room'

WHEN? HOW OFTEN?

abends	in the evenings
ab und zu	now and then/from time to time
am Donnerstagvormittag	on Thursday morning
am Freitagnachmittag	on Friday afternoon
am nächsten/folgenden Tag	the next/following day
am Samstagabend	on Saturday evening
am Wochenende	at the weekend
gestern	yesterday
heute	today
immer	always
jeden Tag	every day
meistens	mostly/mainly
montags	on Mondays
morgen	tomorrow
morgens	in the mornings
nach der Schule	after school
nachmittags	in the afternoons
nie	never
normalerweise	normally/usually
oft	often
selten	rarely/seldom/hardly ever
übermorgen	the day after tomorrow
vorgestern	the day before yesterday

TIMES

um — at

gegen — towards, about

um wieviel Uhr? — at what time?

halb sieben — half past six

Mitternacht — midnight

Viertel nach sieben — quarter past seven

zehn vor sechs — ten to six

zehn Uhr — ten o'clock

zehn nach zwei — ten past two

Mittag — midday

Viertel vor zwei — quarter to two

Examiner's Top Tip

Try learning these expressions of time/frequency alphabetically, as they are here, or as pairs (e.g. opposites: immer – nie) or in groups (e.g. all those that end in -s: morgens, abends, montags, meistens, etc.). Find the way that suits you best, then use lots of them in your spoken and written German.

ROUTINE ROUTINE ROUTINE!

Masculine	Feminine	Neuter
Fruchtsaft (fruit juice)	Freizeit (free time)	Butterbrot (sandwich)
Kuchen (cake)	Hausaufgabe (homework)	Fleisch (meat)
Orangensaft (orange juice)	Kantine (canteen)	Frühstück (breakfast)
Schultag (school day)	Kleidung (clothing)	Mittagessen (lunch)
Tee (tea)	Mahlzeit (meal)	Obst (fruit)
Wecker (alarm clock)	Uniform (uniform)	Wasser (water)

duschen	to shower
kochen	to cook
der Wecker klingelt um ...	the alarm clock rings at ...
putzen	to clean
schlafen	to sleep
trinken	to drink
ich muss eine Uniform tragen	I have to wear a uniform
ich verlasse das Haus gegen acht Uhr	I leave home at about eight o'clock

MORGENS

Ich stehe normalerweise um sechs Uhr auf. Das finde ich zu früh!
I normally get up at six o'clock. I think that's too early!

Erstens dusche ich dann frühstücke ich. Meistens esse ich nichts aber ich trinke gern ein Glas Orangensaft.
I shower then I have breakfast. Most of the time I don't eat anything but I like to drink a glass of orange juice.

Ich ziehe meine Uniform an – die finde ich hässlich – dann verlasse ich das Haus gegen acht Uhr.
I put my uniform on – I think it looks ugly – then I leave home around eight o'clock.

Ab und zu fahre ich mit dem Bus oder mit der Straßenbahn zur Schule. Meistens gehe ich aber zu Fuß.
Occasionally I take the bus or the tram to school. But most of the time I walk.

Ich komme in der Schule um halb neun an. Wir haben nämlich Unterricht um Viertel vor neun.
I get to school at eight-thirty. Lessons begin at a quarter to nine.

Zuerst haben wir zwei Stunden dann machen wir eine kleine Pause, eine Viertelstunde oder so. Dann ist noch Unterricht bis halb eins. Das ist ziemlich lang.
First we have two lessons then we have a short break of about a quarter of an hour. Then it's lessons until 12.30. That's quite a long time.

DAILY ROUTINE 2

NACHMITTAGS

Ich esse nicht gern in der Kantine. Das Mittagessen in der Schule schmeckt mir nie gut. Ich bringe jeden Tag Butterbrote mit.
I don't like eating in the canteen. School dinner never tatses good to me. I take sandwiches to school every day.

Dann haben wir nochmal Unterricht: noch drei Stunden. Eine Stunde dauert fünfundvierzig Minuten. Der Schultag ist um halb vier zu Ende.
Then we've got lessons again: three more lessons. A lesson lasts forty-five minutes. School ends at half past three.

Nach der Schule treffe ich mich mit meinen Freunden im Stadtzentrum. Wir essen ein Eis oder trinken eine Cola.
After school I meet my friends in the town centre. We have an ice cream or a cola.

Ich komme um fünf Uhr wieder nach Hause. Ich ruhe mich aus, dann mache ich meine Hausaufgaben.
I get home at five o'clock. I have a rest, then I do my homework.

ABENDS UND AM WOCHENENDE

Meine Eltern kommen um halb sieben wieder nach Hause. Normalerweise essen wir um halb acht.
My parents get home at 6.30 p.m. We normally eat at 7.30 p.m.

Manchmal koche ich das Abendessen, wenn ich nicht zu viele Hausaufgaben habe.
Sometimes I do the cooking, if I don't have too much homework.

Abends gehe ich selten aus. Ich lese meine Zeitschriften, sehe fern oder höre meine CDs an. Ich gehe um zehn Uhr ins Bett.
I hardly ever go out in the evening. I read my magazines, watch TV or listen to CDs. I go to bed at ten o'clock.

Am Wochenende ruhe ich mich aus oder ich gehe mit meinen Freunden aus.
At the weekend I relax or I go out with my friends.

QUICK TEST

Say/write it in English:

1. Ich stehe um Viertel vor acht auf.

2. Wann gehst du ins Bett?

3. Ab und zu kocht er.

4. Fährst du mit dem Bus oder mit der Bahn zur Schule?

Say/write it in German:

5. First, I wake up early.

6. At what time do you leave home?

7. I rarely have breakfast but I drink a glass of milk.

8. I get bored in school.

9. We have five hours of lessons. I think that's quite a long time!

10. I often listen to CDs in the evening or I go to bed early.

10. Abends höre ich oft CDs an oder ich gehe früh ins Bett.
9. Wir haben fünf Stunden (Unterricht). Das finde ich ziemlich/ganz lang!
8. Ich langweile mich in der Schule/im Unterricht
7. Selten frühstücke ich/esse ich das Frühstück, ich trinke aber ein Glas Milch
6. Um wieviel Uhr verlässt du das Haus?
5. Erstens/Zuerst wache ich früh auf.
4. Do you take/Are you taking the bus or the train to school?
3. He does the cooking now and again.
2. When do you go/are you going to bed?
1. I get up at 7.45 a.m.

SCHOOL AND FUTURE PLANS ❶

SCHOOL SUBJECTS

Fremdsprachen Foreign Languages

Deutsch   **Englisch**

Spanisch   **Französisch**

Naturwissenschaft Science

Bio(logie)

Physik

Chemie

DSP (= darstellendes Spiel)

Erdkunde

Geschichte

Hauswirtschaft

Informatik

Mathe(matik)

Musik

Kunst

Religion

Sport

Werken

Examiner's Top Tip
Try to use these 'qualifiers' with your adjectives, to make what you say/write more interesting and earn more marks:

sehr — very
nicht sehr — not very
ziemlich — quite, fairly
ein bisschen — a bit
wirklich — really
ganz } — completely
total }

SCHOOL LIFE

Note: Plurals are given in brackets. (-) means the word does not change in the plural.

MASKULINUM

Lehrer (-)	teacher (male)
Schüler (-)	pupil (male)
Schuldirektor (-en)	headteacher (male)
Fußballplatz (-plätze)	football pitch
Sportplatz (-plätze)	sports ground
Informatikraum (-räume)	IT room
Schulhof (-höfe)	playground
Schultag (-e)	school day
Stundenplan (-pläne)	school timetable

NEUTRUM

Abitur	exam equivalent to A-Levels/Highers
Fach (Fächer)	school subject
Wahlfach (-fächer)	option/optional subject
Gymnasium (Gymnasien)	equivalent of grammar school
Klassenzimmer (-)	classroom
Lehrerzimmer (-)	staffroom
Labor (-s)	science lab

PLURAL

Hausaufgaben	homework

FEMININUM

Lehrerin (-nen)	teacher (female)
Schülerin (-nen)	pupil (female)
Schuldirektorin (-nen)	headteacher (female)
Gesamtschule (-n)	equivalent of comprehensive school
Oberschule (-n)	equivalent of sixth-form college
Oberstufe (-n)	equivalent of sixth-form
Realschule (-n)	equivalent of secondary school
Privatschule (-n)	private school
Aula (Aulen)	hall
Bibliothek (-en)	library
Klassenarbeit (-en)	test
Fahrt (-en) } Reise (-n) }	journey
(Mittags) pause (-n)	(lunch) break
Prüfung (-en)	exam
Stunde (-n)	lesson
Tafel (-n)	blackboard/ whiteboard
Turnhalle (-n)	gym/sports hall

MORE ADJECTIVES

SCHULFÄCHER	(SCHOOL SUBJECTS)	LEHRER	(TEACHERS)
interessant	interesting	freundlich	friendly
einfach ⎫		nett ⎫	
leicht ⎭	easy	sympathisch ⎭	nice, kind
langweilig	boring	launisch	moody
doof	stupid	streng	strict
schwer	difficult, hard	toll	great, fantastic
furchtbar	terrible, awful	verrückt	mad
super	great, fantastic	Man kriegt mit ihm/	He's/she's great
Ich bin...	I am...	ihr viel Spaß	fun/a laugh
(nicht) (sehr) gut in...	(not) (very) good at...		
Ich bin zu blöd dazu	I'm rubbish at it		

MAGIC MODALS

'Modals' is the name for a group of six really useful verbs:

können	*can*
sollen	*ought to, meant to*
müssen	*must, have to*
mögen	*like*
dürfen	*allowed to*
wollen	*want*

können	sollen	müssen	mögen	dürfen	wollen
k	s	m	m	d	w
n	i	a	o	o	o
o	x	g	d	e	n
w		i	a	s	d
i		c	l		e
n			s		r
g					s

You met five of these modals on page 12, where the parts of those verbs are also listed. The parts of the sixth one, mögen, are:

ich mag	*wir mögen*
du magst	*ihr mögt*
er/sie/es mag	*Sie mögen*
	sie mögen

Modals are nearly always used in sentences with another (main) verb. The second verb:
* *stays in the infinitive*
* *goes to the end of the sentence, e.g.*

MODAL	SECOND VERB

Musst du eine Schuluniform <u>tragen</u>?
Do you have to wear a uniform?

Ich will in die Oberstufe <u>gehen</u>.
I want to go into the sixth form.

Wir dürfen im Klassenzimmer nicht <u>essen</u>.
We are not allowed to eat in the classroom.

NEGATIVES

NICHT
* You use <u>nicht</u> ('not') to make a verb negative.
* If the verb has no direct object, <u>nicht</u> comes straight after the verb.

e.g. Der Lehrer ist <u>nicht</u> sehr nett.
The teacher's not very nice.
Ich bin <u>nicht</u> im Basketballverein.
I'm not in the basketball club.

* But if the verb has a direct object, <u>nicht</u> usually comes straight after the object.

e.g. Ich finde Mathe <u>nicht</u> interessant.
I don't find maths interesting.

* If there is more than one verb (e.g. a modal – see left – and an infinitive), <u>nicht</u> comes just before the <u>second</u> <u>verb</u>.

e.g. Wir dürfen in der Schule <u>nicht</u> rauchen.
We're not allowed to smoke at school.

KEIN
* The Germans use <u>kein</u> instead of <u>nicht</u> <u>ein</u>.
* <u>Kein</u> changes its endings according to the <u>gender</u> and <u>case</u> of the noun it refers to (see page 16).
* The endings on <u>kein</u> are the same as those for <u>ein</u>.

e.g. Die Schule hat kein Schwimmnbad.
The school doesn't have a (has no) swimming pool.
Wir dürfen keine Bonbons im Unterricht essen.
We are not allowed eat sweets in lessons.

SCHOOL AND FUTURE PLANS 2

MEINE SCHULE

Ich besuche eine große Gesamtschule. Wir haben ungefähr tausend Schüler und Schülerinnen und fünfzig Lehrer und Lehrerinnen.
I go to a big comprehensive school. We have around one thousand pupils and fifty teachers.

Sie ist ziemlich modern, aber etwas hässlich.
It's quite modern but rather ugly.

Wir haben eine Turnhalle und eine kleine Bibliothek, aber leider kein Schwimmbad.
We have a sports hall and a small library, but unfortunately no swimming pool.

Ich besuche diese Schule seit fünf Jahren.
I've been going to this school for five years.

Meine Schule gefällt mir gut, weil ich mich mit meinen Freunden dort treffe ...
*I like my school, because I meet up with my friends there ...

... aber wir bekommen zu viele Hausaufgaben!
... but we get too much homework!

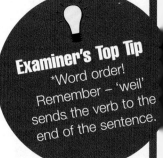

Examiner's Top Tip
*Word order! Remember – 'weil' sends the verb to the end of the sentence.

FÄCHER UND LEHRER

Sag mir etwas über deine Fächer und Lehrer.
Tell me about your subjects and teachers.

**Dieses Jahr muss ich neun Fächer lernen, darum darf ich mich selten ausruhen.
This year I have to study nine subjects, so I can't relax very often.

Ich lerne Englisch, Mathe ...
I do English, maths ...

Was ist dein Lieblingsfach?
What's your favourite subject?

*Mein Lieblingsfach ist Geschichte, weil der Lehrer sympathisch ist.
My favourite subject is history, because the teacher's nice.

Mein bestes Fach ist Chemie, aber ich bin auch gut in Biologie.
My best subject is chemistry, but I'm also good at biology.

*Ich finde Erdkunde langweilig und ich mag Physik nicht, weil die Lehrerin zu streng ist.
I find geography boring and I don't like physics because the teacher's too strict.

Examiner's Top Tip
**By adding a few extra elemen to a sentence, you can earn m marks! In this sentence, 'Dies Jahr', 'darum' and 'selten', p the use of two modals ('mu and 'darf') all help to make strong impression. But ma sure you get the word order right.

MEIN SCHULTAG

Kannst du einen typischen Schultag beschreiben?
Can you describe a typical school day?

Ich fahre mit dem Rad zur Schule.
I come to school by bike.

Es braucht zwanzig Minuten und ich komme gegen Viertel vor neun an. Der Unterricht beginnt um neun Uhr.
It takes twenty minutes and I arrive at about a quarter to nine. Lessons begin at nine o'clock.

Es gibt sieben Stunden pro Tag und wir haben eine Pause um halb elf. Sie dauert fünfzehn Minuten.
There are seven lessons a day and we have a break at half past ten. It lasts fifteen minutes.

Die Mittagspause ist um Viertel nach zwölf. Ich treffe mich mit meinen Freunden im Schulhof. Meistens trinke ich eine Cola und esse Brot mit Käse oder Schinken, Chips und Obst.
The lunch break is at 12.15. I meet my friends in the playground. I usually eat sandwiches with cheese or ham, crisps and fruit.

Die Schule ist um halb vier aus. Ich bin im Computerverein und gehe oft nach der Schule in den Informatikraum, wo ich Internet surfe.
School finishes at half past three. I'm in the computer club and I often go to the computer room after school, where I surf the Internet.

Ich spiele auch für die Fußballmannschaft meiner Schule und wir haben jeden Mittwoch Training von vier bis sechs Uhr.
I also play for the school football team and we have practice every Wednesday from 4.00 to 6.00.

SCHULREGELN

•*Was für Regeln gibt es in deiner Schule und was hältst du davon?*
What rules are there in your school and what do you think of them?

•*Erstens müssen wir alle Schuluniform tragen. Sie ist dunkelgrün und furchtbar. Die Jungen sollen einen Schlips tragen und die Mädchen sollen einen Rock tragen. Das finde ich doof und altmodisch.*
First of all, we all have to wear a school uniform. The boys are supposed to wear a tie and the girls are supposed to wear a skirt. I find that silly and old fashioned.

•*Man darf nicht in der Schule rauchen und Alkohol und Drogen sind strengstens verboten. Meiner Meinung nach ist das gut – so etwas kann gefährlich sein.*
We're not allowed to smoke in school and alcohol and drugs are strictly forbidden. In my opinion, that's good – such things can be dangerous.

ZUKUNFTSPLÄNE

Was willst du nach den Prüfungen machen?
What do you want to do after your exams?

Nächstes Jahr hoffe ich, in die Oberstufe zu gehen. Ich will Englisch, Französisch und Deutsch als Wahlfächer lernen.
Next year I'm hoping to go into the sixth form. I want to study English, French and German as my chosen specialist subjects.

Ich verlasse die Schule und suche einen Job. Ich möchte Automechaniker werden. Ich will Geld verdienen!
I'm leaving school and looking for a job. I'd like to be a motor mechanic. I want to earn some money!

Keine Ahnung! Es kommt auf meine Prüfungsresultate an!
No idea! It depends on my exam results!

Examiner's Top Tip
You can use the present tense to talk or write about future plans, but if you want to make a really good impression and gain more marks, you should use the future tense (see page 84).

QUICK TEST

Say/write it in English:
1. Wir haben ungefähr sieben hundert Schüler und Schülerinnen.
2. Es gibt acht Stunden pro Tag.
3. Meine Lieblingsfächer sind Kunst und Werken.
4. Wir dürfen im Schulhof nicht rauchen.

Say/write it in German:
5. We have to wear a tie.
6. I travel by bus to school.
7. The lunch break is at a quarter to one.
8. I don't like history, because the teacher's too strict.
9. We are not allowed to eat in the classroom.
10. Next year I'm hoping to go into the sixth form.

10. Nächstes Jahr hoffe ich, in die Oberstufe zu gehen.
9. Wir dürfen im Klassenzimmer nicht essen.
8. Ich mag Geschichte nicht, weil der Lehrer/die Lehrerin zu streng ist.
7. Die Mittagspause ist um Viertel vor eins.
6. Ich fahre mit dem Bus zur Schule.
5. Man muss einen Schlips tragen.
4. We are not allowed to smoke in the playground.
3. My favourite subjects are art/design and technology.
2. There are eight lessons a day.
1. We have approximately 700 pupils.

Speaking

Role Play 1
You are arranging to go out with your German friend.
- Ask him/her what (s)he is going to do after school. (1 mark)
- Say you have to do your homework. (1 mark)
- Suggest going out on Friday evening. (1 mark)
- Say you can meet up at 8.00 p.m. in the town centre. (1 mark)

(4 marks)

Role Play 2
You are talking to your German friend about your school life.
- Say how you travel to school. (1 mark)
- Explain what you do at lunchtime. (1 mark)
- Say whether you are in any clubs or teams at school. (1 mark)
- Ask your friend whether (s)he has to wear a school uniform. (1 mark)

(4 marks)

General Conversation

1. Hast du Haustiere? (1 mark)
2. Sag mir etwas über deine Familie. (1 mark)
3. Kommst du mit deiner Familie gut aus? Warum (nicht)? (1 mark)
4. Kannst du deine Mutter oder deinen Vater beschreiben? (Choose one) (1 mark)
5. Was machst du in der Freizeit? (1 mark)
6. Wo wohnst du? (1 mark)
7. Kannst du dein Haus oder deine Wohnung beschreiben? (Choose one) (1 mark)
8. Wie ist dein Schlafzimmer? (1 mark)
9. Sag mir etwas über deine tägliche Routine. (1 mark)
10. Wie ist deine Schule? (1 mark)
11. Welche Fächer lernst du und wie findest du sie? (1 mark)
12. Was für Schulregeln hast du und was hältst du davon? (1 mark)

(12 marks)

Writing

1. Your German friend is doing a survey on what young people would like in their ideal bedroom. Complete the list in German, giving four more items.

Beispiel	Lampe
1	
2	
3	
4	

2. You have received an email from your German friend, Stefan. He wants to know about the school subjects you do, what your teachers are like, the number of lessons you have, after-school activities and your school uniform.

Schreib einen Brief auf Deutsch. Beantworte folgende Fragen:
- Welche Fächer lernst du? (2 marks)
- Welches Fach lernst du nicht gern? (2 marks)
- Warum? (2 marks)
- Wie findest du deine Lehrer? (2 marks)
- Wie viele Stunden hast du pro Tag? (2 marks)
- Was kannst du nach der Schule machen? (2 marks)
- Wie ist deine Schuluniform? (2 marks)
- Stell eine Frage über Stefans Schultag. (2 marks)

(16 marks)

Reading

1. You and your family are looking at the small ads section of a German newspaper. They ask you to help them understand these pieces of information:

Verloren: Wellensittich	a) What type of pet has been lost? (1 mark)
Möchten Sie Klavier spielen?	b) What musical instrument is mentioned here? (1 mark)
Neue Wohnung, fünf Zimmer, Stadtmitte	c) Give two pieces of information about this flat. (2 marks)
Zu verkaufen: Kleiderschrank, Schreibtisch und Teppich	d) Name one thing that is for sale. (1 mark)

(5 marks)

2. Sieh dir folgende Berufe an:

A. Arzt   E. Kellner
B. Lehrerin   F. Kassierer
C. Polizistin   G. Mechaniker
D. Zahnärztin   H. Briefträgerin

Verbinde die Berufe und die Bilder.
Beispiel: 1B

 1.   2.    3.   4.

5.   6.   7.   8.

(7 marks)

3. Lies folgenden Text

Ich heiße Sarah und bin siebzehn [1] alt. Es gibt sechs Personen in [2] Familie. Meine Eltern sind geschieden und ich wohne mit [3] Vater. Meine Mutter ist [4] aber er ist [5]. Ich habe zwei Schwestern und [6] Bruder. Ich komme mit ihm gut aus. Er ist sehr nett aber ein bisschen [7]. Wir [8] zusammen mit dem Rad zur Schule. Am Wochenende [9] wir einkaufen.

Schreib die passenden Buchstaben.
Beispiel: 1G
A. das
B. Deutscher
C. einen
D. fahren
E. faul
F. gehen
G. Jahre
H. Katze
I. meinem
J. meiner
K. Türkin

(8 marks)

How did you do?

1–20	correct	start again
21–35	correct	getting there
36–49	correct	good work
50–60	correct	excellent

IN TOWN

MASKULINUM

Nominative = der/ein,
Accusative = den/einen
Dative = dem/einem

Bahnhof (-höfe)

Busbahnhof (-höfe)

Campingplatz (-plätze)

Dom (e)

Flughafen (-häfen)

Fluss (Flüsse)

Hafen (Häfen)

Kreisverkehr (-)

Markt (Märkte)

Park (s)

Platz (Plätze)
(Marktplatz
= market place square)

See (n)

Strand (Strände)

Turm (Türme)

Wohnblock (-blöcke)

FEMININUM

Nominative
and Accusative = die/eine,
Dative = der/einer

Ampel (n)

Bank (Bänke)

Brücke (n)

Fußgängerzone (n)

Jugendherberge (n)

Kirche (n)

Kreuzung (en)

Polizeiwache (n)

Post (en)

(Reparatur)werkstatt
(-stätten)

Straße (n)
(Hauptstraße =
main road/high street)

Tankstelle (n)

NEUTRUM

Nominative and Accusative =
das/ein, Dative = dem/einem

Einkaufszentrum (en)

Gebäude (n)

Hotel (s)

Kino (s)

Krankenhaus (-häuser)

Monument (e)

Museum (Museen)

Verkehrsamt (-ämter)

Verkehrsbüro (s)

Rathaus (-häuser)

Reisebüro (s)

Schloss (Schlösser)

Schwimmbad (-bäder)
(Freibad = outdoor pool
Hallenbad = indoor pool)

Sportzentrum (en)

Stadion (Stadien)

Theater (s)

SIGNS AND NOTICES

Raucher

Nichtraucher

Zutritt Verboten

Abfahrt

Ankunft

Auskunft

DIRECTIONS AND TRANSPORT ①

THE IMPERATIVE

The imperative is used to give directions, instructions or orders:

Nehmen Sie die erste Straße rechts.
Take the first street on the right.
Geh über die Brücke.
Go over the bridge.

As there are three words for 'you' in German – du, ihr and Sie (see page 9) – there are three ways of giving instructions. The most important to learn are the 'du' form and the 'Sie' form'.

'DU' FORM
• Take the 'du' form of the verb in the present tense and knock off the -st ending:
du gehst → geh* (go)
du nimmst → nimm (take)
• Verbs which take an umlaut in the 'du' form drop this in the imperative:
du fährst → fahr (travel, go)

* an 'e' is sometimes added to regular verbs, e.g. du kommst → komme! but the 'e' is usually left off – komm! (come)

'SIE' FORM
• To make the 'Sie' form imperative of a verb, simply switch 'Sie' and the verb around:
Sie gehen (you go) →
Gehen Sie (go)
Sie nehmen (you take) →
Nehmen Sie (take)

SEPARABLE VERBS
In the imperative, the prefix on separable verbs goes to the end of the sentence:
Steigen Sie ein! (Get in!)
Komm bald zurück! (Come back soon!)

REFLEXIVE VERBS
Reflexive verbs in the imperative keep their reflexive pronoun, e.g. Setz dich!/Setzen Sie sich! (Sit down!)

Reflexive separable verbs have both a reflexive pronoun and a prefix, e.g. Ruh dich aus!/Ruhen Sie sich aus! (Rest!)

'Sein' (to be) is the only verb which is irregular in the imperative:
Sei nicht so blöd!/Seien Sie nicht so blöd! (Don't be so stupid!)

SEPARABLE VERBS

You met some key separable verbs on page 20. You will need to use separable verbs when you are talking about travelling, buying tickets, etc. Here are some important ones:

· abfahren	to depart, leave
· ankommen	to arrive
· einsteigen	to get in
· aussteigen	to get out
· umsteigen	to change (buses, trains, etc.)
· zurückkommen	to come back

When you use separable verbs in sentences, the prefix separates from the main verb. In the present tense, the prefix goes to the end of the sentence:

· Wann fährt der Zug ab?	When does the train leave?
· Steigen Sie hier ein.	Get in here

However, if you use a modal verb (see page 25), the prefix and the main verb stay together and the whole separable verb goes to the end of the sentence:

· Muss ich umsteigen?	Do I have to change?
· Sie steigen in Köln um.	You change in Cologne.
· Wann kommen Sie zurück?	When are you coming back?
· Ich will am Montag zurückkommen.	I want to come back on Monday.
· Darf ich bitte aussteigen?	May I get out, please?

ATHLETIC ACCUSATIVE AND DOSSING DATIVE

· Some prepositions are always followed by the dative (see page 16).
· Some prepositions can be followed by either the dative, or the accusative. They are:

an	to, at, on	*auf	on
hinter	behind	*in	in
neben	next to	über	over, above
unter	under, below	vor	in front of
zwischen	between		

*These prepositions merge with the definite article in the accusative or the dative, to form words such as: 'ans', 'aufs', 'ins' (accusative + das) 'am', 'im', 'zum' (dative + dem) and 'zur' (dative + der) (see page 16).

* If any movement towards something or someone is involved, use the accusative.
* If you are describing position (no movement), use the dative.
One way of remembering this rule is:
Athletic accusative, dossing dative!

Accusative (movement towards)
Wir müssen in den Bus einsteigen.
We must get on the bus.
Fahren Sie über die Ampel.
Go (drive) across the traffic lights.

Dative (position)
Das Kino ist am Marktplatz.
The cinema is in the market square.
Fahren Sie links an der Ampel.
Turn left at the traffic lights
(NB. There is movement, but the sentence describes a position — at the lights)

Examiner's Top Tip
Try learning this rap to remember the prepositions which can take either the accusative or the dative:
Unter, über, neben, an,
Position – use the dative, man!
Zwischen, hinter, in, auf, vor,
Motion's what the accusative's for

ON A JOURNEY

Abfahrt	departure(s)
Ankunft	arrival(s)
Auskunft	information (office)
Ausgang	exit
Notausgang	emergency exit
Eingang	entrance
Ausstieg	exit (to bus, train or plane)
Einstieg	entrance (on bus, train or plane)
Fahrplan (-pläne)	timetable
Fahrschein (e)	ticket
Einfachkarte	single ticket
Rückfahrkarte	return ticket
Fahrkartenschalter	ticket office/ticket window

Fahrkartenautomat	ticket machine
Fahrstuhl/Aufzug	lift
Flugsteig	airport gate
Gepäck	luggage
Gepäckaufbewahrung	left luggage office
Gepäckschließfach (fächer)	left luggage locker
Gleis (en)	platform
Treppe	stairs
Rolltreppe	escalator
Wartesaal	waiting room
Zollkontrolle	customs
Zuschlag	supplement
drücken	(to) push
ziehen	(to) pull

AUF DER STRAßE

Entschuldigung. Wie *komme ich am besten **zum Dom/zur Jugendherberge/zum Schloss, bitte? → *Excuse me. What's the best way to get to the cathedral/youth hostel/castle, please?*

Ist hier in der Nähe ein Campingplatz/eine Post/ein Verkehrsamt, bitte? → *Is there a campsite/post office/tourist information office nearby, please?*
Wo ist der nächste Park/die nächste Bank/das nächste Hotel, bitte? → *Where is the nearest park/bank/hotel, please?*

Er/sie/es ist neben der Kirche. Gehen Sie diese Straße entlang dann um die Ecke und am Ende der Straße gehen Sie links. → *It's next to the church. Go along this street, then around the corner and at the end of the road, turn left.*
Dann gehen Sie über den Schillerplatz und Sie sehen ihn/sie/es gegenüber dem Reisebüro. → *Then cross Schiller Square and you'll see it opposite the travel agents.*

Das ist ganz weit von hier. Am besten nehmen Sie den Bus/die Straßenbahn/die U-Bahn. → *It's quite far from here. The best thing would be to take the bus/tram/underground.*
Wo ist die nächste Haltestelle/der nächste U-Bahnhof, bitte? → *Where is the nearest bus/tram stop/underground station, please?*
Gehen Sie geradeaus an der Post vorbei und sie/er ist auf der rechten Seite. → *Go straight on, past the post office and it's on your right.*

AN DER HALTESTELLE/ IN DER U-BAHN

Examiner's Top Tip
*Only use 'kommen' if you are on foot! If you are in a car (or travelling by any other form of transport), use 'fahren' for 'to go', e.g. Wie fahre ich am besten zum/zur...?

**If you are asking the way to a country, town or village, use 'nach', not 'zu', e.g. Wie fahre ich am besten nach Berlin?

Entschuldigung, mit welcher Linie fährt man zum Schloss, bitte? → *Excuse me, which line goes to the castle, please?*
Linie 56. Steigen Sie am Busbahnhof aus. → *Line 56. Get out at the bus station.*
Wann fährt der nächste Bus, bitte? → *When is the next bus, please?*
Sie fahren alle zehn Minuten ab. → *They leave every ten minutes.*
Entschuldigen Sie. Ist hier der Bus für das Schloss? → *Excuse me. Is this the right bus for the castle?*

Entschuldigen Sie. Welche Richtung ist es zum Flughafen, bitte? → *Excuse me. Which direction is it to get to the airport, please?*
Nehmen Sie Richtung Stadtmitte und steigen Sie am Hauptbahnhof um. → *Take the town centre direction and change at the main station.*
Wo kaufe ich einen Fahrschein/eine Fahrkarte? → *Where can I buy a ticket?*
Entweder am Automat oder am Schalter dort drüben. → *Either at the machine or at the ticket window over there.*
Danke sehr. → *Thank you very much.*

Entschuldigung. Wo steigt man für das Rathaus heraus? → *Excuse me. Where do I get out for the town hall?*
An der nächsten Haltestelle/Station. → *At the next stop/station.*

AM BAHNHOF/AM FLUGHAFEN

Guten Tag. Ich möchte heute/morgen/nächsten Montag nach Hamburg fahren. →
Hello. I'd like to travel to Hamburg today/tomorrow/next Monday.

Gibt es einen Zug/einen Flug gegen zehn Uhr? →
Is there a train/flight at around ten o'clock?

Ja, es gibt einen, der fährt um zehn Uhr fünfundzwanzig ab. →
Yes, there's one that leaves at 10.25.

Wann kommt er an? Muss ich umsteigen? →
When does it arrive? Do I have to change?

Er kommt um zwölf Uhr fünfzehn an. Nein, er fährt direkt. →
It arrives at 12.15. No, it's direct.

Darf ich einen Platz reservieren, bitte? →
Can I book a seat, please?

Einfach oder hin und zurück?/Eine einfache Karte oder eine Rückfahrkarte? →
Single or return?

Hin und zurück, bitte. →
Return, please.

Wann kommen Sie zurück? →
When are you coming back?

Ich komme am Dienstag nachmittag gegen siebzehn Uhr zurück. →
I'm coming back on Thursday afternoon, at around 5 p.m.

Raucher oder Nichtraucher? →
Smoking or non-smoking?

Nichtraucher. Was kostet das, bitte? Muss ich einen Zuschlag zahlen? →
No smoking. How much is it, please? Do I have to pay a supplement?

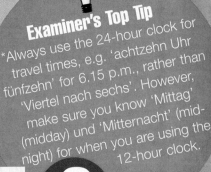

Von welchem Gleis/Flugsteig fährt der Zug/Flug nach Hamburg, bitte? →
Which platform/gate is it for the Hamburg train/flight, please?

Gleis/Flugsteig 12. →
Platform/Gate 12.

Fährt er pünktlich ab? →
Is it leaving on time?

Es tut mir leid. Er hat fünfzehn Minuten Verspätung. →
I'm sorry. It's delayed by 15 minutes.

Wo ist der Wartesaal, bitte? →
Where's the waiting room, please?

DIRECTIONS AND TRANSPORT 2

Examiner's Top Tip
*Always use the 24-hour clock for travel times, e.g. 'achtzehn Uhr fünfzehn' for 6.15 p.m., rather than 'Viertel nach sechs'. However, make sure you know 'Mittag' (midday) und 'Mitternacht' (midnight) for when you are using the 12-hour clock.

QUICK TEST

Say/write it in English:
1. Gehen Sie über die Brücke dann an dem Rathaus vorbei.
2. Fahr bis zur Ampel und es ist auf der linken Seite.
3. Der nächste Zug fährt um zweiundzwanzig Uhr.
4. Der Flug nach München fährt vom Flugsteig Nummer siebzehn ab.

Say/write it in German:
5. Take the first road on the right.
6. Excuse me, how do I get to the police station, please?
7. Is there a post office nearby, please?
8. When does the next tram leave, please?
9. A return to Freiburg, for tomorrow, please.
10. From which platform does the train for Cologne leave?

10. Von welchem Gleis fährt der Zug nach Köln, bitte?
9. Einmal nach Freiburg hin und zurück/Eine Rückfahrkarte nach Freiburg, für morgen, bitte.
8. Wann fährt die nächste Straßenbahn, bitte?
7. Ist hier in der Nähe eine Post, bitte?
6. Entschuldigung/Entschuldigen Sie, wie komme/fahre ich am besten zur Polizeiwache, bitte?
5. Nehmen Sie/Nimm die erste Straße rechts.
4. The Munich flight leaves/departs from gate number 17.
3. The next train leaves at 10 p.m.
2. Go to the traffic lights and it's on the left-hand side.
1. Cross the bridge and then go past the town hall.

TOURISM 1

WORD ORDER

You have already seen how in German the main verb is usually in second place (though not always second word):
Nächste Woche <u>fahre</u> ich nach Deutschland.
I am <u>going</u> to Germany next week
Wohin <u>fährst</u> du in Urlaub?
Where are you <u>going</u> on holiday?

There are other important differences in German word order, such as adverbs of time, manner and place, which you have probably learnt as <u>Time-Manner-Place</u>. Think of them as the three logical stages of a trip:
· Stage One is about <u>when</u> you go, e.g. Nächste Woche (next week), Im August (in August), um acht Uhr (at eight o'clock).
· Stage Two is about <u>how</u> you go, e.g. zu Fuß (on foot), mit dem Zug (by train), alleine (alone), mit meinen Eltern (with my parents).
· Stage Three is about <u>where</u> you go, e.g. nach Köln (to Cologne), in die Alpen (to the Alps), ans Meer (to the seaside)

If you want to get there, too, always stick to this order, making sure that the verb is in its proper place, and you'll score high marks:

1	2	3
Diesen Sommer	fahren wir mit dem Auto	nach Griechenland.
This summer	we're going by car	to Greece.

Heute abend gehe ich mit meiner Freundin ins Kino.
This evening I'm going with my girlfriend to the cinema.

Here's a list of the when, how and where for you to refer to:

1 ➡ WHEN

im April/August/Dezember	in April/August/December
im Frühling/Sommer/Herbst/Winter	in spring/summer/autumn/winter
diesen Sommer	this summer
nächstes Jahr	next year
an Ostern	at Easter
in den Sommerferien	in the summer holidays
zu Weihnachten	at Christmas

2 ➡ HOW

mit dem Flugzeug/Reisebus/Boot/Rad	by plane/coach/boat/bike
mit meinen Cousinen/Eltern/Freunden	with my cousins/parents/friends
mit der Schule	with school
alleine	alone/on my own

3 ➡ WHERE

nach Spanien/Bayern/München/Wien	to Spain/Bavaria/Munich/Vienna
ans Land/Meer/Mittelmeer	to the countryside/seaside/the Mediterranean
in die Alpen/Berge	to the Alps/the mountains
zur Ostsee/Nordsee	to the Baltic/North Sea

Examiner's Top Tip
Remember the verb (must) come first when you (ask) certain questions. Fährst du in Urlaub? Are you going on holiday?

CARNIVAL

Um elf Uhr am 11. November beginnt die Karnevalszeit.
At eleven o'clock on 11 November Carnival time begins.

In Köln feiert man Karneval am Rosenmontag.
In Cologne they celebrate carnival time on the Monday before Lent.

Es gibt Kostümsfeste und Faschingsbälle.
There are costume parades and dances for Lent.

Es gibt auch Umzüge durch die Straßen.
There are also processions through the streets.

Die Leute im Umzug tragen bunte Kostüme und werfen den Zuschauern Bonbons und Blumen zu.
The people in the procession wear colourful costumes and throw sweets and flowers to the spectators.

AT THE TOURIST OFFICE

Wo ist hier das Verkehrsamt, bitte?
Where's the tourist office, please?

Ich möchte einige Infos (über) ...
I'd like some information (about) ...

Haben Sie Prospekte/Broschüren (darüber)?
Have you got brochures (about them)?

**Was gibt es hier zu sehen?
What is there to see here?

In der Stadtmitte.
In the town centre.

Kann man einen Stadtbummel/eine Stadtrundfahrt machen?
Can you can go on a trip round town?

Wo kann man Fahrräder ausleihen?
Where can you hire bikes?

Gibt es hier eine Jugendherberge?
Is there a youth hostel here?

MASCULINE

Campingplatz	campsite
Prospekt	brochure
Rhein	Rhine (river)
Stadtbummel	stroll round town
Stadtplan	town plan
Tourist	tourist
Urlaub	holiday

FEMININE

Auskunft	information
Broschüre	brochure
Fahrkarte	ticket
Hotelliste	list of hotels
Information	information
Rundfahrt	round trip
Sehenswürdigkeit	tourist attraction

NEUTER

Eiscafé	ice-cream bar
Kino	cinema
Museum	museum
Reisebüro	travel agency
Restaurant	restaurant
Verzeichnis	guide
Theater	theatre

Examiner's Top Tip

** The expression 'Es gibt' 'There is', is followed by the accusative case, so if you're describing facilities/amenities you'll need:
'einen' for masculine singular nouns:
Es gibt einen Park There's a park
'eine' for feminine singular nouns:
Es gibt eine Disco There's a disco
'ein' for neuter singular nouns:
Es gibt ein tolles Eiscafé
There's a great ice cream bar.

HOLIDAY PREFERENCES

Ich mache lieber einen Campingurlaub/Skiurlaub/ Sporturlaub.
I prefer camping holidays/skiing holidays/sports holidays.

Ich faulenze gern am Strand.
I like lazing on the beach.

Etwas Interssantes für Jugendliche.
Something interesting for young people.

Nichts gefährliches.
nothing dangerous.

Am liebsten mache ich Ausflüge.
I like going on excursions best.

WEATHER PREFERENCES

Wie ist das Wetter (in)?
What's the weather like (in)

Normalerweise/Oft/Meistens ist es ganz
Usually/Often/Mostly it's quite

nass/neblig/sonnig/
wet/misty/sunny/

stürmisch/windig/ wolkig
stormy/windy/cloudy

es donnert/friert/regnet/ schneit
it thunders/freezes/rains/snows

es ist schön warm/heiß
it's nice and warm/hot

BALD SIND FERIEN!

Bald sind Ferien – toll! Ich freue mich schon darauf.
It's the holidays soon - great! I'm really looking forward to it.

↓

Fährst du in Urlaub oder bleibst du hier zu Hause?
Are you going away or staying here at home?

↓

Was?! Hier bleiben! Das ist nichts für mich! Wir fahren immer in Urlaub.
What?! Stay here! That's not for me! We always go on holiday.

↓

Wohin denn? Mit wem? Und wann?
Where to? Who with? And when?

↓

So viele Fragen! Wir machen eine Pauschalreise: ich fliege Anfang August mit meiner Familie nach Mallorca.
So many questions! We're going on a package holiday: at the beginning of August I'm flying to Majorca with my family

↓

Nach Mallorca? Das ist schön. Für wie lange denn?
To Majorca? That's nice. For how long?

↓

Wir verbringen** drei Wochen in einem Hotel im Süden.
We'll be spending three weeks in a hotel in the south.

↓

Was macht ihr denn dort drüben? Ausflüge? Wanderungen?
What will you do there? Trips? Walks?

Examiner's Top Tip
**Note how you can use the present tense to talk about eve plans or intentions in the nea future, as in English: here you co equally well say 'We're spending three weeks in a hotel'.

Aber nein! Natürlich kann man interessante Ausflüge machen und im Norden kann man selbst Wanderungen im Gebirge machen, aber das mache ich nicht gern.
Of course not! Obviously you can go on interesting excursions and in the north you can even walk in the mountains, but I'm not interested in that.

↓

Schade! Was machst du denn?
That's a shame! What will you do then?

↓

Am liebsten faulenze ich am Strand. Man kann auch Wassersport treiben: Wasserski laufen, segeln, windsurfen – Alles, was!
What I like best is lounging on the beach. You can do watersports, too: water skiing, sailing, windsurfing – the lot!

↓

Wie ist das Wetter im August in Mallorca?
What's the weather like in Majorca in August?

↓

Unglaublich schön! Die Sonne scheint den ganzen Tag, es ist immer heiß und es regnet nie. Abends ist es besonders warm und angenehm.
Unbelievably beautiful! The sun shines all day long, it's always hot and it never rains. In the evenings it's especially warm and pleasant.

WAS FÜR EINEN URLAUB MÖCHTEST DU?

Das ist alles schön und gut aber sowas interessiert mich nicht.
That's all well and good but I'm not interested in that sort of thing.

Ehrlich?! Was für einen Urlaub möchtest du?
Honestly?! What sort of a holiday would you like?

Ich fahre lieber* ans Land oder in die Berge, weil es ganz ruhig aber auch ganz schön ist**.
I prefer going to the countryside or into the mountains because it's quite relaxing but also quite beautiful.

Aber das ist nichts für Jugendliche!
But that's not for young people!

Wieso? Bergsteigen oder Wandern ist besser als* Wasserski laufen. Es gibt zu viel Lärm und zu viele Touristen am Strand und in Stadtmitten. Das kann ich nicht leiden!
What do you mean? Mountain climbing or walking in the country is better than water skiing. There's too much noise and too many tourists on the beach and in town centres. I can't stand that!

Schade! Du willst also nicht nach Mallorca mitkommen?
What a shame! You don't want to come to Majorca with us, then?

Nein danke. Ich bleibe nämlich zu Hause. Ich muss Geld sparen: nächstes Jahr möchte ich in die Alpen fahren.
No, thanks. As a matter of fact I'm staying at home. I have to save up: next year I'd like to go to the Alps.

Examiner's Top Tip

*Use lieber, meaning 'rather', 'preferably' and besser als meaning 'better than' to talk about your preferences in holidays, food, sports, etc. See pages 58–59 for more information on comparatives and superlatives.
**weil, meaning 'because' is another word that changes the word order in a clause (a sentence within a sentence): it sends the verb to the end. Try using it yourself when expressing your opinions.

TOURISM 2

QUICK TEST

Say/write it in English:
1. Fährt sie in Urlaub?
2. Oft ist es sonnig in Mallorca.
3. Sie verbringen zwei Wochen mit ihren Freunden in der Schweiz.
4. Zu Weihnachten bleibe ich immer mit meiner Familie zu Hause.

Say/write it in German:
5. Do you have a list of hotels?
6. Where can you hire bikes?
7. Is there a sports centre?
8. What is there to see here?
9. He prefers travelling by car to Spain.
10. Next week I'm flying to Greece with my parents.

1. Is she going on holiday?
2. It's often sunny in Majorca.
3. They're spending/going to spend two weeks with their friends in Switzerland.
4. I always stay at home with my family after Christmas.
5. Haben Sie eine Hotelliste?
6. Wo kann man hier Fahrräder ausleihen?
7. Gibt es (hier) ein Sportzentrum?
8. Was gibt es hier zu sehen?
9. Er fährt lieber mit dem Auto nach Spanien.
10. Nächste Woche fliege ich mit meinen Eltern nach Griechenland.

ACCOMMODATION 1

RELATIVE PRONOUNS

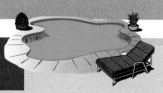

Relative pronouns are used to save time by not repeating the same noun. For example, instead of saying 'I'm looking for a campsite. A campsite that has a swimming pool', you can get rid of the repeated noun <u>campsite</u> (Campingplatz) and replace it with its pronoun:

I'm looking for a campsite that has a swimming pool.
Ich suche einen Campingplatz, <u>der</u> ein Freibad hat.

Examiner's Top Tip
* Remember: the subject of a sentence or a clause, is the person or thing who/that does the action in the verb.
** The direct object of a sentence or clause has the action in the verb done directly to it.

To use relative pronouns correctly, you must following these three steps:
1. Spot the repeated noun (e.g. <u>campsite</u>) and work out if it is <u>masculine</u>, <u>feminine</u> or <u>neuter</u> and decide whether it's <u>singular</u> or <u>plural</u>. In the example above <u>Campingplatz</u> is <u>masculine singular.</u>
2. When you have worked out whether your pronoun is a person (<u>who</u>) or a thing (<u>that</u>, <u>which</u>), look at the clause it's in (e.g. <u>that</u> has a swimming pool) and work out if it is the <u>subject</u>* of the clause or the <u>direct object</u>** of the clause.
3. Always put the verb at the end of its clause.

Here's a diagram to help you remember:

Is the pronoun (repeated noun) the subject?	→	der	die	das (singular)
			OR	
			die (plural)	

Is the pronoun (repeated noun) the direct object?	→	den	die	das (singular)
			OR	
			die (plural)	

| Whatever pronoun you use | → | Send the verb the end of its clause |

Examiner's Top Tip
Be even more impressive by showing your knowledge of the relative pronoun in the dative case:
Die Empfangsdame, der ich gesprochen habe, war sehr hilfsbereit.
The (woman) receptionist I spoke to (to whom I spoke) was very helpful.

CAMPSITES AND YOUTH HOSTELS

Haben Sie noch Platz?	Do you have any room/spaces available?
Was kostet das?	How much is it?
pro Stunde/Tag/Nacht	per hour/day/night
inbegriffen/inklusive	included/all-in prices
Kann man Schlafsäcke ausleihen?	Can you hire sleeping bags?

Masculine		**Feminine**		**Neuter**	
Platz	place, pitch	Jugendherberge	youth hostel	Fahrrad	bike
SB-Laden	self-service shop	Sanitäranlage	wash block	Freibad	open-air pool
Schlafsack	sleeping bag	Übernachtung	overnight/single night	Restaurant	restaurant
Spielraum	games room			Trinkwasser	drinking water
Wohnwagen	caravan	Unterkunft	accommodation	Zelt	tent
		Waschmaschine	washing machine		

HOTELS

MASCULINE		FEMININE		NEUTER	
Balkon	balcony	Dusche	shower	Badezimmer	bathroom
Empfang	reception	Halbpension	half board	Bettuch	sheet
Fahrstuhl	lift	Mehrwertsteuer	VAT	Doppelzimmer	double room
Flur	lobby, entrance hall	Rechnung	bill	Einzelzimmer	single room
		Reservierung	reservation	Familienzimmer	family room
Gang	course (of a meal)	Seife	soap	WC	toilets
		Vollpension	full board		
Schlüssel	key				
Speisesaal	dining room				
Stock	floor (of a building)				

Haben Sie noch Zimmer frei?	Have you got any rooms left/available?
Ich möchte/wir möchten	I'd/we'd like
Ich habe ein Zimmer reserviert	I've booked a room
mit Bad	with a bath(room)
Für zwei Nächte	for two nights
vom zweiten bis zum achten Juni	from 2 to 8 June
Ist das mit Frühstück?	Is breakfast included?
Ich nehme es	I'll take it
Wo ist die Garage?	Where is the garage?
Zahlen, bitte	I'd like to pay, please

PREPOSITIONS: DATIVE CASE

Remember to use these to say where facilities or people are. As you will be using them to state where someone or something is (i.e. in a fixed position), they will generally be followed by the dative case:

MASCULINE AND NEUTER SINGULAR = DEM	FEMININE SINGULAR = DER
am (an dem)	an der
im (in dem)	in der
auf dem	auf der
gegenüber dem	gegenüber der
hinter dem	hinter der
vor dem	vor der

am Schwimmbad	*next to/by the swimming pool*
auf der Terrasse	*on the terrace*
auf dem Balkon	*on the balcony*
im ersten/zweiten/dritten Stock	*on the first/second/third floor*
im Erdgeschoss	*on the ground floor*
in der Jugendherberge	*in the youth hostel*
vor/hinter dem Hotel	*in front of/behind the hotel*
gegenüber dem Restaurant	*opposite the restaurant*

PROBLEMS AND COMPLAINTS

Ich will mich beklagen/beschwerden.
I want to make a complaint.

Der Kleiderschrank ist kaputt.
The wardrobe is broken.

Unser Zimmer ist schmutzig.
Our room is dirty.

Niemand hat uns das Zimmer aufgeräumt.
No one has cleaned our room.

Wir haben keinen Fernsehapparat.
We haven't got a television set.

Es gibt weder Badetücher noch Seife im Badezimmer.
There's neither towels nor soap in the bathroom.

Die Gäste nebenan machen zu viel Lärm.
The people in the room next to us make too much noise.

IM HOTEL

Guten Tag. Wir haben ein Familienzimmer reserviert.
Hello. We've booked a family room.

Wie ist der Name, bitte?
And your name, please?

Thomas. Für fünfzehn Tage.
Thomas. For a fortnight.

Ja, alles in Ordnung, Herr Thomas. Mit Bad oder Dusche?
Yes, that's fine, Mr Thomas. Do you want a room with a shower or a bath?

Mit Dusche. Was kostet das Zimmer?
A shower. How much is the room?

Fünfunddreißig Euros die Nacht. Das Zimmer ist im vierten Stock gegenüber dem Fahrstuhl.
Thirty-five euros per night. The room is on the fourth floor opposite the lift.

Danke. Ist das mit Frühstück?
Thank you. Is breakfast included?

Leider nicht*. Das Frühstück kostet zehn Euros pro Person.
I'm afraid not. Breakfast costs ten euros per person.

Examiner's Top Tip

*By adding asides and fillers, such as <u>leider nicht</u>, you will make your German sound more authentic.
Try some of these:
alles klar   okay, agreed, understood
das stimmt   that's right
das macht   it doesn't matter
doch nichts
das ist mir egal   I'm not bothered

PROBLEME

Guten Morgen, Herr Thomas. Was ist los?
Good morning, Mr Thomas. What's wrong?

Alles, was. Erstens gibt es weder heißes Wasser noch saubere Badetücher im Zimmer.
Everything – Firstly, there's neither hot water nor clean towels in our room.

Was? Ehrlich? Einen Augenblick mal....
What, really? Just a moment....

... und zweitens ist die Seife, die wir im Waschbecken gefunden haben, schon gebraucht worden.
.... and secondly the soap that we found in the wash basin has already been used.

Ach, Herr Thomas, es tut mir furchtbar leid, aber ...
Oh, I'm terribly sorry, Mr Thomas, but ...

Und was noch schlimmer ist, unser Bett ist kaputt und die Tür schließt gar nicht!
And what's even worse, our bed is broken and the door doesn't even lock!

Machen Sie sich keine Sorgen ... aber was machen Sie, Herr Thomas?
Don't worry about it ... what are you doing, Mr Thomas?

Was meinen Sie denn? Wo befindet sich der Campingplatz in dieser Stadt?
What do you think? Where's the campsite in this town?

AM CAMPINGPLATZ

• Guten Tag. Haben Sie noch Platz frei?
Hello. Have you got any space available?

• Das kommt daranf an. Für einen Wohnwagen oder ein Zelt?
That depends. For a caravan or a tent?

• Für ein Zelt, das wir leider nicht mithaben! Kann man hier ein Zelt verleihen?
For a tent that we haven't got with us unfortunately! Can you hire tents here?

• Ja, sicher, kein Problem! Bitte schön, Platz Nummer einundvierzig, dort drüben, sehen Sie, in der Ecke hinter dem Kinderspielplatz.
Yes, of course, no problem! There you are, pitch forty-one over there, can you see it, in the corner behind the children's play area.

• Danke schön. Wir sind drei Personen. Für vierzehn Tage.
Thank you very much. There are three of us. For fourteen days.

• Na, klar. Das wäre also ein Zelt, ein Auto und drei Personen. Das kostet fünfzehn Euros pro Tag.
That's fine. So, that's one tent, one car and three people. That will be fifteen euros per day.

• Hoffentlich ist heißes Wasser auch im Angebot!
I hope that includes hot water!

• Ja freilich! Der Platz ist modern ausgestattet mit beheizten Sanitäranlagen. Wir haben sogar ein Schwimmbad, das auch beheizt ist, ein Restaurant und eine Disko!
Yes, of course! The campsite is fitted with modern equipment and heated wash blocks. We've even got a swimming pool that is also heated, a restaurant and a disco!

ACCOMMODATION ②

QUICK TEST

Say/write it in English:

1. Ist das mit Frühstück?

2. Es gibt weder ein Restaurant noch ein Schwimmbad im Hotel.

3. Ich möchte ein Einzelzimmer im Erdgeschoss.

4. Da ist der Schlüssel, den ich verloren habe.

Say/write it in German:

5. You can hire bikes here.

6. There's no dining room in the hotel.

7. My room is opposite the restaurant.

8. We'd like a single room with a bath.

9. Is it the pitch that's next to the games room?

10. The bike that I hired is broken.

(answers, printed upside-down)

1. Is breakfast included?
2. There's neither a restaurant nor a swimming pool at the hotel.
3. I'd like a single room on the ground floor.
4. That's the key that I lost.
5. Hier kann man Fahrräder ausleihen.
6. Es gibt keinen Speisesaal im Hotel.
7. Mein Zimmer ist gegenüber dem Restaurant.
8. Wir möchten ein Einzelzimmer mit Bad.
9. Ist es der Platz, der am Spielraum ist?
10. Das Rad, das ich ausgeliehen habe, ist kaputt.

Speaking

Role Play 1
You're giving directions to a German tourist in your town:
- Say: bus route number 55. (1 mark)
- Tell him/her to get out at the railway station. (1 mark)
- Tell him the castle is behind the cathedral.(1 mark)
- Say they (i.e. buses) leave every ten minutes.(1 mark)
(4 marks)

Role Play 2
You are talking to a hotel receptionist in Germany:
- Ask if there are any rooms available. (1 mark)
- Say you'd like a family room for five nights. (1 mark)
- Say you'd like a room with a shower. (1mark)
- Ask if breakfast is included. (1 mark)
(4 marks)

General Conversation

1. Was für einen Urlaub machst du am liebsten? (1 mark)
2. Warum denn? (1 mark)
3. Fährst du dieses Jahr in Urlaub oder bleibst du zu Hause? (1 mark)
4. Wohin fährst du meistens in Urlaub? (1 mark)
5. Wann denn? (1 mark)
6. Für wie lange? (1 mark)
7. Mit wem und wie? (1 mark)
8. Was machst du dort drüben? (1 mark)
9. Was für Sehenswürdigkeiten gibt es? (1 mark)
10. Was gibt es für Jugendliche? (1 mark)
11. Wie ist das Wetter normalerweise? (1 mark)
12. Was gibt es für Jugendliche in deiner Stadt? (1 mark)
(12 marks)

Writing

1. You have been asked to send an email to a campsite in Germany.
   Schreib folgende Sätze auf Deutsch:
- I'd like to book a pitch for ten days in August. (2 marks)
- There are three of us and a car and a caravan. (2 marks)
- Is there a swimming pool on the campsite? (2 marks)
- In the name of Jones. How much will it cost? (2 marks)

(8 marks)

2. You have received a letter from your German friend, Claudia. She wants to know all about your holiday preferences. Answer her questions and ask her the question at the end.
   Schreib einen Brief auf Deutsch. Beantworte folgende Fragen:
- Fährst du lieber im Sommer oder im Winter in Urlaub? (2 marks)
- Warum denn? (2 marks)
- Fährst du lieber mit deinen Eltern? (2 marks)
- Was für Sportarten treibst du am liebsten, wenn du auf Urlaub bist? (2 marks)
- Was machst du dieses Jahr während der Ferien? (2 marks)
- Stell ihr eine Frage über ihre Ferienpläne.(2 marks)

Reading

1. Sieh dir folgende Schilder an:

   A Dom   E Campingplatz
   B Museum   F Fluss
   C Schloss   G Einkaufszentrum
   D See

Verbinde die Schilder und die Bilder:
Beispiel: 1B

 1.  2. 3. 4. 5.

(4 marks)

2. Lies folgenden Text:

Ich [1]⃞ gern hier in Altstadt, weil die See und das [2]⃞ ganz in der Nähe sind. Es gibt nicht viel für [3]⃞ in der [4]⃞ , aber man kann am [5]⃞ faulenzen oder sich sonnen. Es ist eine kleine alte Stadt, die auch einen schönen [6]⃞ hat, wo man jeden Tag in den Sommerferien [7]⃞ aus aller Welt [8]⃞ kann. Es ist meine ideale [9]⃞ .

Schreib die passenden Buchstaben.
Beispiel: 1D

A. Hafen	E. Stadt	I. Land
B. sehen	F. Strand	J. Stadtmitte
C. Fluss	G. Touristen	K. Jugendliche
D. wohne	H. besuche	

(8 marks)

3. Lies folgenden Text

Werbung: Winterferien im Hotel Alpenhorn

Leider sind die Sommerferien längst vorbei…. Sie sind müde und bald ist Weihnachten. Sie verbringen die Weihnachtsferien lieber zu Hause, auch wenn Sie keine Lust haben, die ganze Zeit in der Küche zu sein oder sich den ganzen Tag um die Kinder zu kümmern, die auch todmüde sind. Das ist nichts für Sie! Was können Sie denn machen? Ganz einfach! Kommen Sie zum Hotel Alpenhorn, wo die Sonne stundenlang scheint! Treiben Sie gern Wintersportarten? Machen Sie gern Ausflüge? Nichts Einfacheres! Sie sind mitten in den Alpen, und zwar ist die Schweiz auch nicht weit entfernt. Bleiben Sie lieber im Hotel, weil Sie faulenzen möchten? Der Hoteldirektor Herr Schultz bietet Ihnen folgende Luxusdienste: beheiztes Schwimmbad, Fitness-Raum, Satellit-Fernsehen. Und wenn die Sonne nicht scheint, ist es auch kein Problem: fragen Sie Herrn Schultz, der Ihnen jede Menge aussergewöhnliche Aktivitäten vorschlagen kann. Warten Sie keine Minute länger! Reservieren Sie beim Hotel Alpenhorn. Wir wünschen Ihnen schöne Winterferien!

Beantworte folgende Fragen auf Deutsch:
a) Welche Jahreszeit ist das? (1 mark)
b) Es sind bald welche Ferien? (1 mark)
c) Wie kann man die Probleme lösen, die man normalerweise zu Weihnachten hat? (1 mark)
d) Wo können die Hotelgäste skifahren? (1 mark)
e) Welches Land ist ganz naheliegend? (1 mark)
f) Wer ist Herr Schultz? (1 mark)
g) Welche Sportarten kann man im Hotel machen? (2 marks)

(8 marks)

How did you do?

1–20	correct	............................start again
21–35	correct	............................getting there
36–49	correct	............................good work
50–60	correct	............................excellent

THE PERFECT TENSE: BEEN THERE, DONE IT

How do you tell whether you, like Mr Perfect, have been there, done it and bought the T-shirt? Simple: just take four steps back in time and check:

1. Has it happened? Is it over? Finished? e.g. I went/have been there, you did/have done it, he (has) bought it

2. Verbs of motion or the verbs 'to be' and 'to stay'? e.g. I went, you've been, he stayed

3. Part 1 = the present tense of sein (to be) for your main verb (i.e. in second place) e.g. Ich bin …(I have …), du bist …(you have …), er ist … (he has …)

4. Part 2 = past participle (what's been done, finished, etc.) at the end of the sentence/clause. e.g. … gegangen (went on foot), … gefahren (went by vehicle), … geblieben (stayed)

All other verbs. e.g. you (have) done …, he (has) bought …

Part 1 = the present tense of haben (to have) for your main verb (i.e. in second place). e.g. du hast … (you have …), er hat … (he has …)

Part 2 = past participle (what's been done, finished, etc.) at the end of the sentence/clause. e.g. …gemacht (done), … gekauft (bought)

So now you can say who did what:
Ich bin dorthin gefahren
I went (have been) there
Du hast es gemacht
You did it.
Er hat das T-shirt gekauft
He bought the T-shirt

'SEIN' VERBS IN THE PERFECT TENSE

Learn Part 1 of these verbs by heart, then look at Part 2 and try to work out the rules for forming the past participle. Check your theory by looking at the guidelines below.

Part 1 (Main verb) sein (to be)	Part 2 (Past participle)	Translation
Ich bin	gewandert	I went walking
du bist	gereist	You travelled
er/sie/es/man ist	geliebeen	He/she/it/we stayed
wir sind	gefahren	We went/travelled
ihr seid	geflogen	You flew
Sie sind	geschwommen	You swam/went swimming
sie sind	angekommen*	They arrived

FORMING PAST PARTICIPLES

Answer the following questions and you'll soon crack the past participle code for 'sein' and 'haben' verbs:

1. Is it a regular/weak verb?
→ Past participle is ge......t, so:
reisen (to travel) → gereist (travelled)
spielen (to play) → gespielt (played)
kaufen (to buy) → gekauft (bought)
wandern (to go walking) → gewandert (went/have been walking)

2. Is it an irregular/strong verb? → Past participle is ge......en, so:
schlafen (to sleep) → geschlafen (slept)
schwimmen (to swim) → geschwommen (went swimming)
essen (to eat) → gegessen (eaten)
bleiben (to stay) → geblieben (stayed)

3. Do you add ge- to all verbs to form the past participle?
No, don't add ge- if they begin with: be-, er-, ge-, ver-, zer- or end in: -ieren

Infinitive	Past Participle	Example
bekommen	bekommen	Was hast du bekommen? (What have you received?)
erreichen	erreicht	Wir haben Berlin erreicht (We've reached Berlin)
gewinnen	gewonnen	Ich habe viel Geld gewonnen (I've won lots of money)
verstehen	verstanden	Er hat nichts verstanden (He understood nothing)
zerreißen	zerrissen	Du hast den Schlafsack zerrissen (You've torn the sleeping bag)
verlieren	verloren	Ich habe meine Schlüssel verloren (I've lost my keys)

Examiner's Top Tip

*If you're using a separable verb like ankommen, make sure the separable prefix e.g. an, mit, auf, etc. is at the front of the past participle:
Sie sind spät angekommen
They arrived late
Wer ist mitgefahren?
Who travelled with you?
Um wieviel Uhr seid ihr aufgestanden?
At what time did you get up?

'HABEN' VERBS IN THE PERFECT TENSE

As with 'sein' verbs in the perfect tense, you should learn Part 1 of these verbs by heart, then look at Part 2. If necessary, look back to the guidelines on the previous page to remind yourself how to form the past participle.

Part 1 (Main verb) haben (to have)	Part 2 (Past participle)	Translation
Ich habe	gespielt	I played
du hast	getanzt	You went bowling
er/sie/es/man hat	gatanzt	he/she/we danced
wir haben	geschlafen	We slept
ihr habt	gesehen	You saw
Sie haben	genommen	You took
sie haben	angerufen*	They telephoned

HOLIDAY ACTIVITIES 1

HOLIDAY ACTIVITIES

Use the expressions below, divided into regular and irregular verbs and expressions, to talk about holiday activities. The past participles are given in brackets.

Regular/Weak Verbs

Ausflüge machen (gemacht)	go on outings
besuchen (besucht)	visit
faulenzen (gefaulenzt)	lounge around, doss
grillen (gegrillt)	have a barbecue
surfen (gesurft)	go surfing
tauchen (getaucht)	go diving
Volleyball spielen (gespielt)	play volleyball

es war toll/fantastisch/langweilig!
it was great/fantastic/boring
es hat mir gut gefallen
I liked/enjoyed it
Das Essen fand ich mies
I thought the food was lousy

Irregular Verbs

essen (gegessen)	eat
Rad fahren (gefahren)	go bike riding
spazieren gehen (gegangen)	go for a walk
Sport treiben (getrieben)	to do sport
viel unternehmen (unternommen)	do lots of things
Wasserski laufen (gelaufen)	go water skiing

Apart from irregular/strong verbs, whose past participles end in -en, there are other, slightly irregular verbs that you will have to learn by heart:
bringen – gebracht (brought)
denken – gedacht (thought)
haben – gehabt (had)
verbringen – verbracht (spent (time))

You should also remember how to use the small number of reflexive verbs, e.g. sich sonnen (to sun one-self/sunbathe):

ich + mich, du + dich, er/sie/es/man + sich
wir + uns, ihr + euch, sie + sich, Sie + sich.
e.g.
ich habe mich gesonnt (I sunbathed)
du hast dich gesonnt (you sunbathed)

Once you have learnt these and all the exceptions to the rule, you will be able to use them to gain high marks, not only with the Perfect tense but also the Pluperfect tense (see page 49).

FOOD FOR THOUGHT

Masculine		Feminine		Neuter	
(Eis)becher	(ice cream) coupe	Bratwurst	(fried) sausage	Bier	beer
Imbiss	snack (bar)	Erdbeere	strawberry	Eis	ice cream
Kuchen	cake	Kirsche	cherry	Getränk	drink
Nachtisch	dessert, pudding	Milch	milk	Glas	glass
Reis	rice	Portion	portion	Mineralwasser	mineral water
Senf	mustard	Sahne	cream	Spiegelei	fried egg
Sprudel	sparkling water	Schokolade	chocolate	Tagesmenü	menu of the day
Wein	wine	Speisekarte	menu		
Zucker	sugar	Suppe	soup		

BIST DU IN URLAUB GEFAHREN?

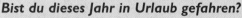

Bist du dieses Jahr in Urlaub gefahren?
• *Did you go on holiday this year?*
Wohin? Wann? Für wie lange? Mit wem? Wie? Was hast du gemacht? Erzähl mal!
• *Where to? When? For how long? Who with? How did you get there? What did you do? Tell me all about it!*

Ich habe drei Wochen mit meinen Eltern in einem Ferienort in Italien verbracht.
• *I spent three weeks with my parents in a holiday resort in Italy.*

Das war in der Nähe von Venedig, direkt an der Küste.
• *It was near Venice, right on the coast.*

Wir sind von Hamburg geflogen. Der Flug hat anderthalb Stunden gedauert.
• *We flew from Hamburg. The flight lasted an hour and a half.*

Examiner's Top Tip
*Remember to make you[r]
sentences interesting by va[rying]
the length, using simpl[e]
conjunctions like und and [...]
expressions of time: d[...]
danach, jeden Tag, a[...]
intensifiers: besonders [...]*

Danach* haben wir ein Auto am Flughafen gemietet, und* sind sofort zum Hotel am Strand gefahren.
• *Then we rented a car at the airport and drove straight to the hotel near the beach.*

Das Wetter war fantastisch – meistens dreißig Grad am Tag, und es hat gar nicht geregnet.
• *The weather was fantastic – thirty degrees usually and it didn't rain at all.*

Wir haben so viel unternommen. Ich habe viel Sport getrieben, besonders* am Strand.
• *We did so much. I did lots of sport, especially on the beach.*

Wir haben jede Menge Ausflüge gemacht – Museen besucht, historische Gebäude besichtigt, Stadtbummel gemacht.
• *We went on loads of outings – visited museums, went to see historical buildings, wandered round town.*

Natürlich konnte ich auch ein bisschen faulenzen. Ich habe mich jeden Tag auf dem Balkon gesonnt, dann bin ich im Schwimmbad geschwommen. Das war toll!
• *Of course, I was able to laze around a bit, too. Every day I sunbathed on the hotel balcony, then I went for a swim in the swimming pool. That was great!*

Ich bin mit meiner Mutter Wasserski gelaufen. Das war komisch, denn ich bin mindestens zehnmal ins Wasser hingefallen.
• *I went water skiing with my mother. That was funny, because I fell in the water at least ten times.*

Was mir aber am besten gefallen hat, war das Tauchen mit meinem Vater.
• *But what I liked best of all was sea diving with my father.*

Ich habe dreimal in der See getaucht. Das war so schön! Bunte Fische und Pflanzen und alles war so still!
• *I went diving three times in the sea. It was so beautiful! Colourful fish and plants and everything was so calm and quiet!*

Das italienische Essen war auch lecker. Schade, dass es nur drei Wochen gedauert hat!
• *The Italian food was delicious, too. It's a shame it only lasted three weeks!*

HOLIDAY ACTIVITIES 2

IM RESTAURANT

Guten Abend. Was darf es sein?
Good evening. What will it be?

Wir haben einen Tisch für zwei Personen reserviert. Mein Name ist Müller.
We've booked a table for two. My name is Müller.

Ach ja, Herr Müller. Einen Tisch neben dem Fenster oder in der Ecke?
Oh yes, Mr Müller. A table by the window or in the corner?

Neben dem Fenster, bitte.... Danke. Haben Sie die Speisekarte?
Near the window.... Thank you. Have you got the menu?

Also, Herr Müller, haben Sie schon bestellt?
Now, Mr Müller, have you placed your order?

Nein, noch nicht. Für mich ein halbes Hähnchen mit grünen Bohnen und Pommes frites.
No, not yet. I'll have a half chicken with green beans and chips.

Also keine Vorspeise? Und für Sie, Frau Müller?
No starter, then? And what about you, Mrs Müller?

Auch keine Vorspeise. Für mich ein Pfeffersteak mit Bratkartoffeln.
No starter for me either. I'd like the pepper steak with fried potatoes.

Möchten Sie etwas dazu trinken?
Would you like something to drink?

Ja. Eine halbe Flasche Rotwein und eine Flasche Mineralwasser.
Yes. Half a bottle of red wine and a bottle of mineral water.

So, hat es Ihnen geschmeckt?
Did you enjoy your meal?

Leider nicht. Das war ekelhaft – kaltes Hähnchen und zähe grüne Bohnen!
Unfortunately not. It was disgusting – cold chicken and tough green beans.

Es tut mir furchtbar leid. Vielleicht könnte ich Ihnen einen Nachtisch empfehlen?
I'm terribly sorry. Perhaps I could recommend a dessert for you?

Sicherlich nicht! Zahlen, bitte!
Certainly not! The bill, please!

QUICK TEST

Say/write it in English:

1. Eine Flasche Bier.
2. Eine Portion Torte mit Sahne, bitte.
3. Ich bin ins Kino gegangen.
4. Er hat Volleyball gespielt.

Say/write it in German:

5. You flew to Berlin.
6. They arrived at ten o'clock
7. Did you go on holiday last year?
8. We spent two weeks in a holiday resort near Naples (Neapel).
9. I sunbathed and did lots of sport.
10. She did too many things.

10. Sie hat zu viel unternommen.
9. Ich habe mich gesonnt und habe viel Sport getrieben.
8. Wir haben zwei Wochen in einem Ferienort in der Nähe von Neapel verbracht.
7. Bist du letztes Jahr in Urlaub gefahren?
6. Sie sind um zehn Uhr angekommen.
5. Du bist (Sie sind/Ihr seid) nach Berlin geflogen.
4. He played volleyball.
3. I went to the cinema.
2. A slice of tart with cream, please.
1. A bottle of beer.

INDIRECT OBJECT PRONOUNS

Pronouns are small words which replace nouns in a sentence:
- Wie geht es <u>deiner Mutter</u>? (How is your mother?) → Wie geht es <u>ihr</u>? ('How is she?')
- Können Sie <u>mir und meiner Familie</u> helfen? (Can you help me and my family?) → Können Sie <u>uns</u> helfen? (Can you help us?)

In the examples above, the pronouns (ihr and uns) are in the dative case

Pronouns in the dative case are called <u>indirect object pronouns</u>.
Here are some further examples:

Kannst du <u>mir</u> ein Aspirin geben?   Can you give me (to me) an aspirin?
Komm mit <u>mir</u>   Come with me
  (dative after the preposition 'mit')
Was ist mit <u>dir</u> los?   What's the matter with you?

Here is a summary of the indirect object pronouns:

Dative (indirect object pronouns)	
mir	uns
dir	euch
ihm	Ihnen
ihr	ihnen
ihm	

LOST AND STOLEN PROPERTY

Ich habe (meine Tasche) verloren — I've lost (my bag)
Haben Sie (sie) gefunden? — Have you found (it)?
Jemand hat (meine Brieftasche) gestohlen — Someone's stolen (my wallet)

Maskulinum (der)
Fotoapparat — camera
Koffer — suitcase
Pass — passport
(Regen)Schirm — umbrella
Ring — ring
Rucksack — rucksack

Femininum (die)
Brille — glasses, spectacles
Tasche — bag
Brieftasche — wallet
Handtasche — handbag
Kreditkarte — credit card
(Armband)Uhr — watch

Neutrum (das)
Fundbüro — lost property office
Gepäck — luggage
Handy — mobile telephone
Portemonnaie — purse

Plural (die)
Schlüssel — keys
Ich habe ihn/sie/es/sie heute morgen im Bus verloren/vergessen/hinterlassen — I lost/forgot/left it/them, this morning on the bus
Er/sie/es ist/sie sind aus ... — It/they are made of ...
Leder — leather
Gold — gold
Silber — silver
Die Marke ist (Sony) — It's a (Sony) brand
Drinnen ist mein Walkman/meine Sonnenbrille/mein Tagebuch — Inside is my personal stereo/my sunglasses/my diary
Drinnen sind meine Kleider/ungefähr fünfzig Euros — Inside are my clothes/about 50 Euros

POST OFFICE, BANK & TELEPHONE

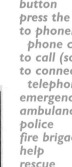

Auf der Post
Maskulinum (der)
Brief (e) — letter
Briefkasten — letter box
(Brief)Umschlag (-schläge) — envelope
Femininum (die)
Briefmarke (n) — stamp
eine Briefmarke zu 65 cent — a 65 cent stamp
Ansichtskarte (n) — picture postcard
Postkarte (n) — blank postcard
Postleitzahl — post code
Neutrum (das)
Paket (e) — parcel, package
Päckchen (-) — small parcel

einwerfen — to post
schicken — to send
eine E-Mail schicken — to send an email
ein Fax schicken — to send a fax
wiegen — to weigh

In der Bank/Im Geldwechsel
Maskulinum (der)
Geldschein (e) — bank note
Geldwechsel — bureau de change
Reisescheck (s) — traveller's cheque
(Wechsel)Kurs — rate of exchange
Femininum (die)
Münze (n) — coin
Sparkasse — savings bank
Unterschrift — signature
Wechselstube — bureau de change
Neutrum (das)
Geld — money
Bargeld — cash
Kleingeld — (loose) change
unterschreiben — to sign
wechseln — to change

In der Telefonzelle
Telefonzelle — telephone box
Hörer — receiver
Den Hörer heben — lift the receiver
Freizeichen — ringing tone
Das Freizeichen aufwarten — wait for the tone
(Telefon)Nummer (n) — telephone number
Vorwahlnummer — dialling code
Die Nummer wählen — dial the number
Telefonkarte (n) — telephone card
Geld oder Telefonkarte einführen — insert money or phone card
Knopf (Knöpfe) — button
Den Knopf drücken — press the button
telefonieren — to phone/make a phone call
anrufen — to call (someone)
verbinden — to connect (by telephone)
Notruf — emergency call
Krankenwagen — ambulance
Polizei — police
Feuerwehr — fire brigade
Hilfe — help
Rettung — rescue

PROBLEMS AND SERVICES ①

ILLNESS AND INJURY

Wie geht es dir/Ihnen?	How are you?
Was ist los?/Was hast du?	What's wrong
Mir ist	I am/I feel
schlecht/warm/kalt	ill/hot/cold
Ich fühle mich nicht wohl	I don't feel well
Ich bin krank/müde	I'm ill/tired
Ich habe	I've got
Bauchschmerzen/ Magenschmerzen	stomach ache
Halsschmerzen	a sore throat
Kopfschmerzen	a headache
Ohrenschmerzen	earache
Rückenschmerzen	backache
Zahnschmerzen	toothache
Durchfall	diarrhoea
Fieber	a temperature/fever
Schnupfen	a cold
einen Sonnenbrand	sunburn
eine Grippe	flu

mein	my (masculine)
Arm/Finger/Fuß	arm/finger/foot
meine	my (feminine)
Hand/Nase	hand/nose
mein	my (neuter)
Auge/Bein/Knie	eye/leg/knee
tut weh	hurts
meine	my (plural)
Augen/Füße	eyes/feet
tun weh	hurt

Ich habe meinen Finger/ meine Hand/mein Bein verletzt/gebrochen	
I have hurt/broken my finger/hand/leg	
Ich habe mich erbrochen	
I've been sick (vomited)	
husten	to cough

(Husten)Saft	(cough) syrup/ mixture
Sirup	syrup
Termin	(doctor's or dentist's) appointment
Pastille (n)	pastille
Tablette (n)	tablet
Salbe	cream, ointment
Medikament	medicine
Rezept	prescription
verschreiben	to prescribe
Arzt/ Ärztin	doctor
Zahnarzt/ Zahnärztin	dentist
Apotheke	chemist's shop

BREAKDOWNS & ACCIDENTS

Was ist los?
What's wrong?
Was ist passiert?
What happened?

BREAKDOWNS
•Können Sie mir bitte helfen?
Can you help me, please?
•Können Sie bitte einen Mechaniker herschicken?
Can you please send a mechanic?
•Ich habe/Wir haben eine Panne.
I/We have broken down.
•Ich habe kein Benzin mehr.

I've run out of petrol.
•Ich habe eine Reifenpanne/Mein Reifen ist geplatzt.
I've got a flat tyre.
•Mein Auto/Motorrad ist kaputt.
My car/motorbike has broken down.
•Die Batterie ist nicht in Ordnung.
The battery's not working.
•Die Bremsen/Die Scheibenwischer sind nicht in Ordnung.
The brakes/windscreen

wipers aren't working.
•Die Windschutzscheibe ist gebrochen.
The windscreen is broken.
•Ich bin auf der Autobahn A8, fünf Kilometer von Stuttgart entfernt, Richtung Stuttgart.
I'm on the A8 motorway, five kilometres from Stuttgart, going towards Stuttgart.
•Mein Auto ist ein roter Volkswagen, Kennzeichen….
My car's a red Volkswagen, registration number…..

ACCIDENTS
•Hilfe!
Help!
•Ich habe/Wir haben einen Unfall gehabt.
I've/We've had an accident.
•Jemand ist/Ich bin verletzt.
Someone's/I am injured.
•Wir brauchen einen Krankenwagen/ die Polizei/die Feurwehr.
We need an ambulance/the police/the fire brigade.
•Haben Sie einen Erste-Hilfe-Kasten?
Do you have a first aid box?

THE PLUPERFECT TENSE

The perfect tense (see page 44) describes what has happened, e.g. Ich habe mein Handy im Restaurant hinterlassen! (I have left my mobile phone in the restaurant!)
The pluperfect tense describes what had already happened, e.g. Ich hatte es auf den Tisch verlegt. (I had put it on the table.)

The pluperfect tense is made of two parts, similar to the perfect tense:
· the imperfect tense of haben or sein (see page 62).
· the past participle of the main verb (see page 44).

Jemand hat meinen Koffer gestohlen.

Someone's stolen my suitcase.

Ich war zum Kiosk gegangen …

I had gone to the kiosk

und hatte ihn auf den Boden gestellt …

… and had put it down …

GELD WECHSELN

Ich möchte etwas Geld wechseln, bitte.
I'd like to change some money, please.

Welche Währung haben Sie, bitte?
Which currency do you have, please?

Pfund. Ich möchte einen Reisescheck zu vierzig Pfund und fünf Pfund Bargeld wechseln.
Pounds. I'd like to change a £40 traveller's cheque and £5 cash.

Haben Sie Ihren Pass, bitte?
Do you have your passport, please?

Das macht siebzig Euros. Wollen Sie bitte hier unterschreiben?
That makes 70 Euros. Can you sign here, please?

VERLOREN, GEFUNDEN!

Hallo, ist das das Hotel Meyer? Hier ist Herr Müller. Können Sie mir helfen, bitte?
Hello, is that the Meyer Hotel? This is Mr Müller. Can you help me, please?

Selbstverständlich. Wo fehlt's?
Of course. What's the problem?

Ich habe meinen Koffer verloren. Habe ich ihn vielleicht in meinem Zimmer hinterlassen?
I've lost my suitcase. Did I perhaps leave it behind in my room?

Ich glaube nicht … Moment mal … Man hat einen Koffer im Fahrstuhl gefunden….
I don't think so … Wait … Somebody found a suitcase in the lift….

Wie ist Ihr Koffer?
What's your suitcase like?

Er ist ziemlich groß und braun, aus Leder.
It's quite big and brown, made of leather.

Darin sind mein Laptop, mein Fotoapparat und meine Kleider.
Inside are my laptop, my camera and my clothes.

Welche Marke sind der Laptop und der Fotoapparat?
What make are the laptop and the camera?

Der Laptop ist ein Toshiba und der Fotoapparat ist ein Canon.
The laptop is a Toshiba and the camera is a Canon.

Machen Sie sich keine Sorgen. Ihr Koffer ist hier.
Don't worry. Your suitcase is here.

AUF DER POST

Guten Tag. Was kosten ein Brief und eine Ansichtskarte nach England, bitte?
Hello. How much are a letter and a postcard to England, please?

Es kostet fünfundsiebzig Cent für einen Brief und fünfundsechzig Cent für eine Ansichtskarte. Wie viele Briefmarken brauchen Sie?
It costs 75 Cents for a letter and 65 Cents for a postcard. How many stamps do you need?

Ich nehme drei Briefmarken zu fünfundsiebzig Cent, bitte.
I'll take three 75 Cent stamps, please.

Ich möchte auch dieses Paket nach Frankreich schicken.
I'd also like to send this parcel to France.

Können Sie es bitte wiegen?
Can you weigh it, please?

Kann man hier telefonieren?
Can I make a phone call from here?

Ja. Die Telefonzellen sind dort drüben.
Yes. The phone booths are over there.

Haben Sie Telefonkarten, bitte?
Do you have telephone cards?

Ja, natürlich. Sie möchten eine Karte zu welchem Wert?
What value of card do you want?

Ich muss auch eine E-Mail schicken. Kann ich das hier tun?
I also have to send an email. Can I do that here?

Leider nicht. Aber es gibt ein Internetcafé gegenüber.
Unfortunately not. But there's an Internet café opposite.

IN DER APOTHEKE

Guten Tag. Ich fühle mich nicht wohl. Ich habe Schnupfen und ich bin sehr müde.
Hello. I feel ill. I've got a cold and I'm very tired.

Haben Sie ein Rezept?
Do you have a prescription?

Nein, ich war noch nicht beim Arzt.
No, I haven't been to the doctor's yet.

Na gut. Haben Sie Kopfschmerzen und Halsschmerzen?
Okay. Have you got a headache and a sore throat?

Ja. Ich habe überall Schmerzen. Besonders im Rücken.
Yes, I ache all over. Especially my back.

Ich glaube, Sie haben auch Fieber.
I think you've also got a temperature.

Ach ja, mir ist warm und ich bin sehr durstig.
Yes, I'm hot and very thirsty.

Meiner Meinung nach, haben Sie eine Grippe. Nehmen Sie diese Tabletten...
In my opinion, you've got the flu. Take these tablets...

...zweimal pro Tag und bleiben Sie im Bett. Wenn es Ihnen nicht besser geht, machen Sie einen Termin mit dem Arzt.
...twice a day and stay in bed. If it doesn't get better, make an appointment to see the doctor.

EIN UNFALL

Na gut, sind Sie die Zeugin? Haben Sie den Unfall gesehen?
Right, are you the witness? Did you see the accident?

Also, ich war an der Ampel angehalten.
Well, I had stopped at the lights.

Ein Auto – das blaue Toyota dort drüben – ist sehr schnell um die Ecke gekommen und ist geschleudert.
A car – the blue Toyota over there – came around the corner very fast and skidded.

Ja. Was ist danach geschehen?
Yes. What happened after that?

Das Auto ist durch den Zaun gefahren und ist mit dem Baum zusammengestoßen.
The car drove through the fence and hit the tree.

Und der Fahrer?
And the driver?

Er war aus seinem Auto ausgestiegen und war auf die Straße hingefallen, bevor ich ihn erreichen konnte.
He had got out of his car and fallen over in the road, before I could reach him.

Er hatte sich den Kopf und die Schulter verletzt.
He had hurt his head and his shoulder.

Dann ist der Krankenwagen gekommen und er ist zum Krankenhaus gefahren worden. Das ist alles, was ich gesehen habe.
Then the ambulance came and he was taken to hospital. That's all I saw.

PROBLEMS AND SERVICES ②

QUICK TEST

Say/write it in English:

1. Ich habe Zahnschmerzen und bin sehr müde.

2. Hier ist ein Rezept. Nehmen Sie diese Tabletten dreimal pro Tag.

3. Jemand hat mein Portemonnaie gestohlen.

4. Ich hatte sie auf den Tisch gestellt.

Say/write it in German:

5. Can you help me? I've got a flat/burst tyre.

6. I've got a cold and a sore throat.

7. I've lost my watch. It's silver.

8. I'd like to send a letter to England, please.

9. I had stopped at the crossroads and I saw the accident.

10. The driver had hurt his leg. I called an ambulance.

10. Der Fahrer hatte sich das Bein verletzt. Ich habe einen Krankenwagen angerufen.
9. Ich war an der Kreuzung gehalten und habe den Unfall gesehen.
8. Ich möchte einen Brief nach England schicken, bitte.
7. Ich habe meine Armbanduhr verloren. Sie ist aus Silber.
6. Ich habe Schnupfen und Halsschmerzen.
5. Können Sie mir helfen? Ich habe eine Reifenpanne.
4. I had put it on the table.
3. Someone has stolen my purse.
2. Here is a prescription. Take these tablets three times a day.
1. I've got toothache and am very tired.

Speaking

Role Play 1
You're in a restaurant in a German speaking country:
• Say you've booked a table for two people.
  (1 mark)
• Say: in the corner, and ask for the menu. (1 mark)
• Order chicken and chips with green beans.
  (1 mark)
• Ask for an orange juice and a mineral water.
  (1 mark)

(4 marks)

Role Play 2
You are at a post office in Germany:
• Ask how much a letter to England costs. (1 mark)
• Say you'd like four 75 cent stamps. (1 mark)
• Say you'd also like to send this parcel to Spain.
  (1 mark)
• Say: can you weigh it, please? (1 mark)

(4 marks)

General Conversation

1. Was hast du letztes Wochenende gemacht? (1 mark)
2. Um wieviel Uhr bist du am Samstagvormittag aufgestanden? (1 mark)
3. Wohin bist du am Samstagabend gegangen? (1 mark)
4. Mit wem bist du geblieben/dorthin gegangen? (1 mark)
5. Was hattest du/hattet ihr am Nachmittag gemacht? (1 mark)
6. Wie war es? (1 mark)
7. Wo hast du deine Sommerferien verbracht? (1 mark)
8. Mit wem bist du in Urlaub gefahren? (1 mark)
9. Wie lange bist du/seid ihr dort geblieben? (1 mark)
10. Wo habt ihr gewohnt? (1 mark)
11. Wie hast du/habt ihr es gefunden? (1 mark)
12. Was für Ausflüge hast du/habt ihr gemacht? (1 mark)

(12 marks)

Writing

1. Your suitcase disappeared from your hotel, while you were on holiday in Frankfurt. The hotel manager has emailed you the following questions about the suitcase, its contents and where you left it:
   Beantworte folgende Fragen auf Deutsch:
   • Was haben Sie verloren? (1 mark)
   • Wo haben Sie ihn verloren? (1 mark)
   • Wie ist er? (Schreib 2 Details auf.) (2 marks)
   • Was war drinnen? (Schreib 2 Details auf.) (2 marks)
   • Beschreiben Sie einen der Gegenstände, die drinnen waren. (2 marks)

(8 marks)

2. Your German friend, Claudia wants to know all about the holiday you spent in Italy last summer. Answer her questions and ask her the question at the end.
   Schreib einen Brief auf Deutsch. Beantworte folgende Fragen:
   • Wohin bist du in Italien gefahren? (2 marks)
   • Mit wem bist du dorthin gefahren? (2 marks)
   • Ihr seid nicht mit dem Auto gefahren, oder? (2 marks)
   • Hast du andere Jugendliche kennengelernt? Wie war es? (2 marks)
   • Was hat dir am besten gefallen? (2 marks)
   • Stell ihr eine Frage über ihren letzten Urlaub. (2 marks)

(12 marks)

Reading

1. Whilst on holiday with your family in Germany, you are asked to explain some of the signs, services and advertisements you come across in the street:

- Magenschmerzen? Nehmen Sie Bauchbonbons!
- Ansichtskarten: 50 Cents
- Fundbüro im Erdgeschoss
- Herr Doktor Schmerz: Zahnarzt
- Wechselstube: 100 Meter geradeaus

- What complaint is 'Bauchbonbons' for? (1 mark)
- What costs 50 Cents? (1 mark)
- What is on the ground floor? (1 mark)
- What does this person do for a living? (1 mark)
- What can be found 100 metres straight ahead? (1 mark)

(5 marks)

2. Lies folgende Werbung:

> Ab Ende Juni: SONDERPREISE
> Schlusselringe. –10%
> Rucksäcke und Regenschirme: –20%
> Lederne Brieftaschen und Handtaschen: –25%
> Fotoapparate: –30%
> Kreditkarten und Reiseschecks werden akzeptiert

Schreib R (Richtig) oder F (Falsch):
1. Die Preise werden im Winter reduziert. (1 mark)
2. Die Preise sind mindestens von zehn Prozent reduziert worden. (1 mark)
3. Die Taschen sind aus Plastik. (1 mark)
4. Es gibt keinen Sonderpreis für Fotoapparate. (1 mark)
5. Man kann mit seiner Kreditkarte zahlen. (1 mark)

(5 marks)

Sicherheitsgürtel oder Unfall?
Vor zwei Monaten war ich mit meiner Familie auf Urlaub in Bayern. Wir hatten einen schönen Ausflug aufs Land gemacht. Leider hatte es begonnen zu regnen, darum hatten wir beschlossen, so schnell wie möglich wieder ins Hotel zurückzukommen. Es war fast dunkel, aber ich habe den Lastkraftwagen klar gesehen. Er ist auf der nassen Straße geschleudert. Dann ist er durch einen kleinen Zaun gefahren und ist mit einem großen Baum gestoßen.

Wir haben die Polizei und den Krankenwagen sofort angerufen, weil der Fahrer sich schwer verletzt hatte. Ich glaube, er hatte sich den Arm gebrochen und er war ohnmächtig. Er hatte sich auch am Kopf verletzt. Das war furchtbar! Zum Glück sind die Feuerwehr und der Krankenwagen erst nach zehn Minuten angekommen. Man hat den Fahrer sehr schnell ins Krankenhaus gefahren. Der Polizist, der mir ein Paar Fragen über den Unfall gestellt hat, hat mir auch gesagt, dass der Fahrer seinen Sicherheitsgürtel nicht anhatte. Darum hatte er sich so schwer verletzt. So eine Dummheit!
Jens-Peter

3. Lies folgenden Artikel:
   Beantworte folgende Fragen auf Deutsch:
   a) Wann und wo war Jens-Peter auf Urlaub? (2 marks)
   b) Wie war das Wetter? (2 marks)
   c) Warum ist der Lastkraftwagen geschleudert? (2 marks)
   d) Was haben Jens-Peter und seine Familie sofort nach dem Unfall gemacht? (2 marks)
   e) Woher weiß Jens-Peter, dass der Lastkraftwagenfahrer seinen Sicherheitsgürtel nicht anhatte? (2 marks)

(10 marks)

How did you do?

1–20	correct	start again
21–35	correct	getting there
36–49	correct	good work
50–60	correct	excellent

PERFECT TENSE OF SEPARABLE VERBS

AUFSCHNEIDEN = TO CUT UP

You will remember that, in the perfect tense, the main verb becomes what is called the past participle and that most past participles start with 'ge': gekauft, gemacht, gegangen, gesehen, etc. You also need an auxiliary verb – haben or sein (see pages 44–45):

You should also remember that separable verbs begin with a small word or prefix – such as 'auf', 'an', 'ab' or 'ein' – and that this prefix separates from the main part of the verb in some sentences.

In the perfect tense, the 'ge' comes between the prefix and the main part of the verb, but stays as one word:

ICH HABE SIE AUFGESCHNITT...

Gestern musste ich meiner Mutter helfen. Ich habe alles für das Abendessen <u>eingekauft</u> und nach dem Essen habe ich <u>abgewaschen</u> und <u>abgetrocknet</u>!
Yesterday, I had to help my mother. I did all the shopping for the evening meal and after the meal I washed up and dried up!

Ist das alles? Ich bin um sieben Uhr <u>aufgestanden</u>, habe mein Zimmer <u>aufgeräumt</u>, meine kleine Schwester von der Ballettklasse <u>abgeholt</u> und bin erst um Mittag <u>ausgegangen</u>. Der Is that all? I got up at seven o'clock, tidied my bedroom, fetched my little sister from her ballet class and only went out at midday.

HELPING AROUND THE HOME

FREQUENCY

jeden Abend/Morgen/Monat/ Samstag/Tag	every evening/morning/month/ Saturday/day
(fast) jede Woche	(almost) every week
jedes Wochenende	every weekend
am Wochenende	at the weekend
abends	in the evening
morgens	in the morning
nachmittags	in the afternoon
gestern	yesterday
gestern Abend	yesterday evening
letztes Wochenende	last weekend
letzten Sonntag/Dienstag (etc.)	last Sunday/Tuesday (etc.)
(nur) ab und zu	(only) now and then, occasionally
immer	always
meistens	mostly
normalerweise	usually
(fast) nie	(almost) never

SEPARABLE VERBS

abholen	to fetch
abspülen }	to wash up
abwaschen }	
abtrocknen	to dry up
aufräumen	to tidy (up)
einkaufen	to do the shopping
den Müll hinausbringen	to take out the rubbish

NON-SEPARABLE VERBS

bügeln	to do the ironing, to iron
den Tisch decken	to lay the table
das Bett machen	to make the bed
den Rasen mähen	to mow the lawn
putzen	to clean
Staub saugen	to do the vacuuming
das Auto waschen	to wash the car
im Garten arbeiten/helfen	to work/help in the garden
mich um (meinen kleinen Brüder) kümmern	to look after (my little brother)
babysitten	to babysit

MEALTIMES

zum Frühstück	**for breakfast**
zum Mittagessen	**for lunch/midday meal**
zum Abendessen	**for dinner/evening meal**
zum Abendbrot	**for tea/supper**
mittags	**at lunchtime/midday**
Ich bin Vegetarier/Vegetarierin	**I'm a vegetarian**

USING 'MAN'

'Man' is used a lot in German.
It takes the same part of the verb as 'er', 'sie' and 'es'
It has several different meanings:
• It can mean 'we', e.g. Abends isst man um halb acht. (In the evenings we eat at 7.30.)
• It can mean 'you', e.g. Was isst man zum Frühstück bei dir zu Hause? (What do you eat for breakfast at home?)
• It can mean 'people', e.g. In Deutschland isst man mittags meistens heiß. (In Germany people usually eat a hot midday meal.)

HOME LIFE 1

PLURAL NOUNS

As most German nouns don't just add an 's' in the plural (like English), it is important to learn the plural along with the singular.

There are some patterns, but there are always exceptions, so be careful! Here are a few general rules:
- Most feminine nouns ending in 'e' add '<u>n</u>' in the plural:
  Geburtstagskarte → Geburtstagskarte<u>n</u>.
- Feminine nouns ending in 'ung', 'keit' and 'heit' add '<u>en</u>' in the plural:
  Mahlzeit → Mahlzeiten.
- Feminine nouns ending in 'in' add '<u>nen</u>' in the plural:
  Vegetarierin → Vegetarierin<u>nen</u>.
- Many masculine words and neuter words add '<u>e</u>' in the plural:
  Tag → Tage/Jahr → Jahre.
- Some masculine and neuter words add an <u>umlaut</u> to the vowel and 'e' or 'er' to the end of the word, in the plural: Baum → Bäume, Haus → Häuser.
- Most masculine and neuter words ending in 'er', 'en' or 'el' stay the same in the plural: Spieler → Spieler, Zimmer → Zimmer.
- Words which come from other languages often add 's' in the plural:
  Hotel → Hotels, Auto → Autos.

Remember

To say 'first', 'second', etc.:
Add -en to all numbers up to 19.
Add -sten to all numbers from 20 to 99.
1st = ersten, 2nd = zweiten,
3rd = dritten
NB. When giving dates, note that you do not need a word for 'of':
Ich habe am achten Dezember Geburtstag.
(My birthday is on the 8th of December.)

CELEBRATIONS

Wann ist es?	When is it?	im Juni/Oktober (etc.)
Es ist …	Its is …	in June/October (etc.)
im	in (the)	am ersten/zweiten/dritten/
Frühling	spring	zweiundzwanzigsten/dreißigsten (etc)
Sommer	summer	Januar/Mai
Herbst	autumn	on the 1st/2nd/3rd/22nd/30th (etc.) of
Winter	winter	January/May

Zu Diwali — For Diwali
Zu Hannukah — For Hannukah
… zündet man Kerzen an
… we / people light candles

man … — we/people …
schenkt … — give (presents) …
schickt … — send …
schmückt … — decorate …
singt … — sing …
wartet auf … (+ accusative) — wait for …
wünscht … — wish …

zu Weihnachten — At Christmas
frohe Weihnachten! — Happy Christmas!

MASKULINUM (DER)
am Heiligabend — on Christmas Eve
am ersten Weihnachtstag — on Christmas Day
Weihnachtsmann — Father Christmas
Sankt Nikolaus — Saint Nicholas
Weihnachtsbaum — Christmas tree

FEMININUM (DIE)
Bescherung — the giving out of presents on Christmas Eve
Weihnachtskarte(n) — Christmas card(s)

NEUTRUM (DAS)
Weihnachtsgeschenk(e) — Christmas present(s)
Weihnachtslied(er) — Christmas carol(s)

das neue Jahr — New Year
das Neujahr — New Year's Day
am Sylvester — on New Year's Eve
man … — we/people …
begrüßt/feiert das neue Jahr — see in/celebrate the New Year
sieht das Feuerwerk an — watch the fireworks
tanzt — dance
trinkt Sekt — drink champagne
hat viel Spaß — have fun
(ein) glückliches/gutes neues Jahr! — Happy New Year!

das Fest(e)	Festival
der Feiertag(täge)	National/public holiday
Karneval/Fasching …	Carnevaltime/Fasching (Shrovetide)
zu Ostern	At Easter
das Osterei(er)	Easter egg

Wann hast du / haben Sie Geburtstag?
When is your birthday?
Ich habe am …(date)…Geburtstag
My birthday's on …
Herzlichen Glückwunsch (zum Geburtstag)!
Happy Birthday!
Ich bekomme Karten und Geschenke
I get cards and presents

das Chinesische Neujahr
Chinese New Year

WILKOMMEN!

Willkommen in Kassel!
Welcome to Kassel!
Wie war die Reise?
How was the journey?
Nicht schlecht, danke. Nur ein bisschen lang.
Not bad, thanks. Just a bit long.
Darf ich dir meine Familie vorstellen?
Can I introduce my family?
Hier ist mein Vater, meine Mutter…
This is my father, my mother…
Freut mich.
Pleased to meet you.
Warst du schon in Deutschland?
Have you been to Germany before?
Ja, ich war vor zwei Jahren auf einer Klassenfahrt in München.
Yes, I went to Munich on a school trip two years ago.

> **Examiner's Top Tip**
> Notice the word order if you want to say 'ago': vor zwei Jahren.

Hier ist dein Schlafzimmer. Brauchst du etwas?
Here's your bedroom. Do you need anything?
Hast du bitte ein Handtuch?
Have you got a towel, please?
Die Handtücher sind in diesem Schrank.
The towels are in this cupboard.
Decken findest du in der Kommode. Es gibt Bücher, Zeitschriften und Comics auf dem Tisch.
You'll find blankets in the chest of drawers. There are books, magazines and comics on the table.
Danke. Das ist sehr nett von dir.
Thanks. That's very kind of you.

Auf Wiedersehen. Vielen Dank für Ihre Gastfreundschaft.
Goodbye. Thanks you for your hospitality.
Nichts zu danken. Gute Reise und komm bald wieder zurück!
Don't mention it. Have a good journey and come back soon!

Normalerweise isst man abends kalt. Das Abendbrot essen wir um acht Uhr.
We usually eat something cold in the evenings. We have supper at eight o'clock.
Ich muss meiner Mutter in der Küche helfen. Kommst du mit?
I must help my mother in the kitchen. Do you want to come with me?
Ja, gerne. Darf ich Ihnen helfen, Frau Schneider?
Yes, I'd like to. Can I help you, Frau Schneider?
Ja, danke. Kannst du bitte den Tisch decken?
Yes, thank you. Can you please lay the table?
Wir brauchen fünf Teller, Messer, Gabeln und Löffel. Oh, und Gläser auch.
We need five plates, knives, forks and spoons. Oh, and glasses, too.
Wie hilfst du deinen Eltern zu Hause?
What do you do to help your parents at home?
Ich spüle immer ab und am Wochenende wasche ich das Auto – dafür gibt mir mein Vater Geld. Letzten Samstag habe ich mein Zimmer aufgeräumt – das muss ich jede Woche tun.
I always do the washing up and at the weekend I wash the car – my father gives me some money for doing that. Last Saturday I tidied my room – I have to do that every week.

> **Examiner's Top Tip**
> Remember to volunteer information in your speaking test and make sure you show that you can use other tenses, not just the present. For a good example, look at this speech.

MAHLZEITEN

Was isst du normaleweise zum Frühstück?
What do you usually have for breakfast?
Meistens esse ich Cornflakes oder Müsli mit Milch und vielleicht Toast mit Butter oder Marmelade. Ab und zu esse ich ein gekochtes Ei. Ich trinke immer Kaffee - Tee schmeckt mir nicht.
Usually I eat cornflakes or muesli with milk and perhaps toast with butter or jam. Occasionally I have a boiled egg. I always drink coffee – I don't like tea.

Und um wieviel Uhr ist das Abendessen?
And when do you have dinner?
In der Woche essen wir gegen sieben Uhr, aber am Wochenende etwas später.
In the week, we eat around seven o'clock, but a bit later at the weekend.
Kannst du ein typisches Essen beschreiben?
Can you describe a typical meal?
Ich bin Vegetarier/Vegetarierin, darum esse ich kein Fleisch und keinen Fisch.
I'm a vegetarian, so I don't eat any meat or fish.
Meine Familie isst Hähnchen oder Bratwurst mit Gemüse.
My family eat chicken or sausages, with vegetables.
Ich nehme lieber Nudeln mit Salat. Zum Nachtisch essen wir alle Joghurt oder Eis.
I prefer pasta with salad. For dessert, we all have yogurt or ice cream.

Mittags isst man meistens kalt oder heiß in Großbritannien?
Do people usually eat hot or cold at midday in Britain?
Das ist verschieden. In der Schulkantine kann man warme Speise - Hamburger, Pizza, Pommes frites, und so weiter - kaufen.
It varies. In the school canteen you can buy hot food – burgers, pizza, chips, etc.
Aber zum Mittagessen esse ich lieber kalt - Butterbrote und etwas Obst.
But at lunchtime I prefer to eat something cold – sandwiches and some fruit.
Abends essen wir heiß zu Hause.
In the evening we have a hot meal at home.

FESTE UND FEIERTAGE

Wie feiert man Weihnachten bei dir? How do you celebrate Christmas at home? Zu Weihnachten, schickt man Weihnachtskarten und schenkt Weihnachtsgeschenke. At Christmas, we send Christmas cards and give Christmas presents. Der Tradition nach isst man Truthahn und Plumpudding. It's traditional to eat turkey and Christmas pudding. In Deutschland schenkt man Geschenke am Heiligabend, aber meistens bei uns schenkt man am ersten Weihnachtstag Geschenke. In Germany, people give presents on Christmas Eve, but normally we give presents on Christmas Day.

Examiner's Top Tip

Remember to use 'du', 'dich' and 'dir' with someone you know well or a young person. Use 'ihr' and 'euch' with more than one person you know well ('ihr' is the plural form of 'du'). Use 'Sie' and 'Ihnen' with any-one you don't know well. If in doubt, use 'Sie' until someone invites you to call them 'du'!

Weihnachten und Ostern feiern wir nicht. Wir sind Juden/Muslims/Hindus. We don't celebrate Christmas and Easter. We are Jewish/Moslems/Hindus. Welches ist das wichtigste Fest für dich? What's the most important festival for you? Das wich-stige Fest für uns ist Hanukkah/Ramadan/Diwali (etc.). The most important festival for us is Hanukkah/Ramadan/Diwali (etc.). Man zündet Kerzen an. Man isst.... We light candles. We eat....

HOME LIFE 2

QUICK TEST

Say/write it in English:

1. Jeden Tag staube ich Saug.

2. Letztes Wochenende habe ich den Rasen gemäht.

3. Vielen Dank für Ihre Gastfreundschaft.

4. Weihnachten ist ein wichtiges Fest in Deutschland.

Say/write it in German:

5. I always do the drying up.

6. Yesterday, I did the shopping.

7. We usually have the evening meal at 7.30

8. For breakfast, I eat toast and drink tea.

9. How do you celebrate Christmas at home?

10. We (people) dance, we sing, we give presents.

10. Man tanzt, man singt, man schenkt Geschenke.
9. Wie feiert man Weihnachten bei dir?
8. Zum Frühstück esse ich Toast und trinke Tee.
7. Meistens/Normalerweise essen wir das Abendessen um halb acht.
6. Gestern habe ich eingekauft.
5. Ich trockne immer ab.
4. Christmas is an important festival in Germany.
3. Thank you for your hospitality.
2. Last weekend I mowed the lawn.
1. I do the vacuuming every day.

COMPARATIVES

You revised the use of adjectives on page 9. Now you can compare two (groups of) things or people, by using the comparative adjective. When they are not directly in front of a noun, comparative adjectives in German are even easier than in English: just add -er to the end, unless it is one of the small number of short adjectives that also add an umlaut.*

Pizza ist <u>billig</u> aber Hamburger sind <u>billiger</u>.
Pizza's <u>cheap</u> but hamburgers are <u>cheaper</u>.

Hamburger sind <u>lecker</u> aber Pizza ist <u>leckerer</u>.
Hamburgers are <u>delicious</u> but pizza is <u>more delicious</u>.

Hamburger sind nicht so lecker wie Pizza.
Hamburgers aren't as delicious as pizza.

MORE THAN THAT!

To make your comparisons even clearer, use <u>als</u> to translate <u>than</u>:
Pizza ist leckerer als Hamburger.
Pizza is more delicious than hamburgers.
If you want to avoid using the comparative but still make comparisons, you can use this negative expression:

nicht so → [+ adjective] → + wie

COMPARATIVES BEFORE NOUNS

As soon as you place the comparative directly before the noun it describes, you have to treat it like any other adjective and change its ending, depending on the gender (masculine, feminine, neuter) and the case (nominative, accusative, genitive, dative) of the noun:

•*Mein älterer Bruder isst lieber Pommes frites.*
My elder brother prefers to eat chips.

•*Die kleineren Portionen machen nicht so unfit.*
The smaller portions don't make you so unfit.

Learn these two tables and you'll find it a lot easier:

'ein' group adjectives

Case	Masculine	Feminine	Neuter	Plural
Nom	mein älterer Bruder	meine ältere Schwester	mein älteres Kind	meine älteren Freunde
Acc	meinen älteren Bruder			
Gen	meines älteren Bruders	meiner älteren Schwester	meines älteren Kinds	meiner älteren Freunde
Dat	meinem älteren Bruder		meinem älteren Kind	meinen älteren Freunden

'der' group adjectives

Case	Masculine	Feminine	Neuter	Plural
Nom	der ältere Bruder	die ältere Schwester	das ältere Kind	die älteren Freunde
Acc	den älteren Bruder			
Gen	des älteren Bruders	der älteren Schwester	des älteren Kinds	der älteren Freunde
Dat	dem älteren Bruder		dem älteren Kind	den älteren Freunden

SUPERLATIVES

To compare more than two (groups of) things or people, you need the superlative adjective, to translate words like 'the tastiest', 'the most expensive':

add -est or -st to the adjective (again very much like the English) and use this formula if the superlative is not directly in front of its noun:

am + adjective ending in -en

e.g. billig → billigst → am billigsten:

Hamburger sind <u>am billigsten</u>.
Hamburgers are the cheapest.

e.g. lecker → leckerst → am leckersten
Pizza ist <u>am leckersten</u>.
Pizza is the most delicious.

For superlatives directly before nouns, follow the rules for comparatives above and add the appropriate endings from the two grids.

Mein älte<u>st</u>er Bruder isst gern Süßes.
My eldest brother likes to eat sweet things.
Die klein<u>st</u>en Portionen sind auch nicht so teuer.
The smallest portions are also less expensive.

Make sure you know these common exceptions:
·gut → der beste, etc., am besten (the best)
·alt → (ältest-) → der älteste, etc., am ältesten (the oldest)
·jung → (jüngst-) → der jüngste, etc., am jüngsten (the youngest)
·groß → (größt-) → der größte, etc., am größten (the biggest)
·kurz → (kürzest-) → der kürzeste, etc., am kürzesten (the shortest)
·lang → (längst-) → der längste, etc., am längsten (the longest)

STAY FIT AND HEALTHY

Um fit zu bleiben	in order to stay fit
man sollte (nicht)	you should (not)
früh aufstehen und früh ins Bett gehen	get up and go to bed early
gesund essen	eat healthy foods
(keinen) Alkohol trinken	drink (no) alcohol
(keine) Drogen nehmen	take (no) drugs
Bist du aktiv?	Do you keep active?
Ich fahre täglich Rad	I cycle every day
Ich schwimme regelmässig	I go swimming regularly
Ich habe aufgehört, zu rauchen	I've given up smoking
Ich trainiere oft	I often go training
Zweimal in der Woche mache ich Aerobik	I do aerobics twice a week

HEALTHY LIVING 1

POSITIVELY NEGATIVE

Ich esse…	I eat
immer	always
alles Gebratene**	everything fried
nie	never
nicht zu viel	not too much
nichts Besonderes**	nothing in particular
nichts Fettiges	nothing greasy/fatty
nichts Süßes	nothing sweet
(kein) Gemüse	(no) vegetables
(kein) Obst	(no) fruit
(kein) Fett	(no) fat
(kein) Fleisch	(no) meat

Examiner's Top Tip
**Show the examiner you know the difference between alles + adjective (with a capital letter and ending in -e), meaning 'everything/all that is…' e.g. alles Leckere (everything that's tasty) and nichts + adjective (again with a capital letter and ending in -es), meaning 'nothing…', e.g. nichts Gebratenes (nothing fried).

YOU ARE WHAT YOU EAT

Maskulinum		Femininum		Neutrum	
Apfel	apple	Ananas	pineapple	Beefsteak	steak
Blumenkohl	cauliflower	Aprikose	apricot	Bier	beer
Bratensaft	frying fat	Birne	pear	Brötchen	bread roll
Essig	vinegar	Butter	butter	Ei	egg
Joghurt	yogurt	Erbse	pea	Fett	fat (in food)
Pilz	mushroom	Hauptspeise	main meal	Gemüse	vegetables
Reis	rice	Pizza	pizza	Kalbfleisch	veal
Salat	salad	Sahne	cream	Rezept	recipe
Schinken	ham	Vegetarierin	vegetarian	Rindfleisch	beef
Vegetarier	vegetarian				

HEALTHY LIVING ②

FEIN UND GESUND ESSEN

Auch Vegetarier können leckere Gerichte essen! Nichts Feineres als gefüllte Aubergine …
Even vegetarians can eat delicious meals! There's nothing finer than stuffed aubergine …

… zur Hauptspeise und Pfannkuchen zum Nachtisch. Und, was noch besser ist, sind beide …
… for your main course and pancakes for dessert. And, even better, both …

… ganz einfach zu kochen. Unten sind die Rezepte. Guten Appetit!
… are simple to cook. The recipes appear below. Enjoy your meal!

GEFÜLLTE AUBERGINE

Zutaten für vier Personen
Vier Auberginen
Vier Esslöffel Margarine
Vier Zwiebeln
Vier Teelöffel Kokosmilch
Vier gewürfelte Tomaten
Curry, Salz, Pfeffer

STUFFED AUBERGINE

Ingredients for four people
Four aubergines
Four tablespoons of margarine
Four onions
Four teaspoons of coconut milk
Four diced tomatoes
curry powder, salt, pepper

Zubereitung
Preparation and cooking

1. Aubergine halbieren*, Fruchtfleisch herauslösen* und klein hacken*.
Cut the aubergines in half, hollow out the flesh and chop it finely.
2. Die Zwiebeln dünsten.*
Stew the onions.
3. Tomaten, Auberginenmark und Kokosmilch dazu und würzen*.
Add the tomatoes, aubergine flesh and coconut milk and season.
4. Masse in die Auberginenhälften, bei 200C circa. 40–50 Minuten backen*.
Bake the mix in the halved aubergines for about 40–50 minutes at 200 degrees Celsius.

PFANNKUCHEN

Zutaten
Drei Tassen Sojamilch
Ein Esslöffel Öl
100 g Obst oder Nüsse,
150 g sehr klein zerdrückter (besser pürierter) Tofu
500 g Mehl,
Salz, Zucker, Zimt

PANCAKES

Ingredients
3 cups of soya milk
1 tablespoon of oil
100 grams of fruit or nuts
150 grams of crushed (preferably pureed) Tofu
500 grams of flour
Salt, sugar, cinnamon

ZUBEREITUNG   PREPARATION AND COOKING
1. Alles zu einem ziemlich dicken Teig zusammenrühren.
Beat everything into a fairly thick batter.
2. In einer heißen Pfanne ziemlich dünn braten.
Fry fairly thin coatings of batter in a hot pan.
3. Einmal wenden.
Turn once.
4. Mit einer Auflage Schokoladensoße oder Honig servieren.
Serve with a topping of chocolate sauce or honey.

Examiner's Top Tip
*Notice how the infinitive is used in recipes to give instructions:
Zutaten vermischen
Mix the ingredients.
Kartoffeln schälen und würfeln
Peel and dice the potatoes.

FIT UND SATT

Wie bleibst du fit? Bist du aktiv?
How do you keep fit? Do you lead an active life?

Ja, ich bin ganz sportlich. Lieber Sport treiben als Fernsehen!
Yes, I'm quite sporty. Better to do sport than watch television!

Was für Sportarten treibst du denn?
What sort of sports do you do, then?

Ich schwimme und trainiere regelmässig, mindestens dreimal in der Woche.
I swim and train regularly, at least three times a week.

Darum bist du so fit! Hast du aber keine schlechten Gewohnheiten? Trinkst du keinen Alkohol zum Beispiel?
That's why you're so fit! But haven't you got any bad habits? Don't you drink any alcohol, for example?

Alkohol trinke ich nicht gern* – ich trinke lieber* Milch und am liebsten* trinke ich Mineralwasser.
I don't like drinking alcohol – I prefer to drink milk and best of all I like drinking mineral water.

Isst du auch keine Hamburger?
Don't you eat hamburgers either?

Für mich ist das noch schlimmer als Alkohol trinken. Das hat kein Geschmack und ist furchtbar fettig. Man sollte nichts Fettiges essen, wenn man fit bleiben will.**
For me that's even worse than drinking alcohol. They have no taste and they're incredibly fatty. You shouldn't eat anything fatty if you want to keep fit.

Was ist dein Lieblingsgericht?*
What's your favourite dish?

Ich habe eigentlich kein Lieblingsgericht. Da ich aber Vegetarier bin, esse ich überhaupt kein Fleisch. Ich esse besonders gern alles Frische: frisches Gemüse, frisches Obst und fast nichts Gebratenes.**
I haven't really got a favourite dish. Since I'm vegetarian, I don't eat meat at all. I particularly like anything fresh: fresh vegetables, fresh fruit, almost nothing fried.

Isst du denn nichts Süßes?
Don't you eat anything sweet?

Doch! Schokolade! Schokoladeneis oder Pfannkuchen mit Schokoladensoße. Das finde ich lecker, wenn nicht besonders gesund!
Oh, yes, I do! Pancakes with chocolate sauce. I think that tastes delicious, even if it's not especially healthy!

Examiner's Top Tip
*gern, lieber, am liebsten. [a]re the comparative and superlative of [ger]n': lieber often translates as 'rather', [pref]erably' or 'better', while am liebsten [onl]y translates as 'favourite' or 'best of [all. Y]ou can also use 'Lieblings-' on the [fr]ont of nouns to say 'favourite': [Pf]annkuchen mit Honig ist mein Lieblingsnachtisch.
[A]Pancake with honey is my favourite dessert.

Examiner's Top Tip
**Remember the subordinating conjunctions like weil (because), that you can use to give opinions and reasons. By showing the examiner you can use them with the correct word order, you'll score heavily in the exams.

QUICK TEST

Say/write it in English:

1. Pfannkuchen sind leckerer.

2. Nichts Billigeres.

3. Hamburger sind am fettigsten.

4. Das ist mein Lieblingsgericht.

Say/write it in German:

5. I'm more active than you.

6. He eats nothing sweet.

7. Do you like eating pizza and chips?

8. Vegetarians shouldn't eat hamburgers.

9. That's worse than eating veal.

10. Mix everything together and bake for thirty minutes.

10. Alles vermischen und dreißig Minuten backen.
9. Das ist noch schlimmer als Kalbfleisch essen.
8. Vegetarier sollten keine Hamburger essen.
7. Isst du gern Pizza mit Pommes frites?
6. Er isst nichts Süßes.
5. Ich bin aktiver als du/Sie.
4. That's my favourite dish.
3. Hamburgers are the fattiest/greasiest.
2. Nothing cheaper.
1. Pancakes are more delicious.

THE IMPERFECT TENSE

Was <u>machtet</u> ihr, als die Marsbewohner gelandet sind?
What <u>were</u> <u>you</u> <u>doing</u> when the Martians landed?

Wir <u>waren</u> zu Hause.
We <u>were</u> at home.

Ich <u>spielte</u> Fußball im Garten.
I <u>was</u> <u>playing</u> football in the garden.

Mein Bruder <u>duschte</u> <u>sich</u>.
My brother <u>was</u> <u>taking</u> a <u>shower</u>.

Meine Schwester <u>kochte</u>.
My sister <u>was</u> <u>cooking</u>.

Meine Eltern <u>sahen</u> <u>fern</u>.
My parents were <u>watching</u> <u>television</u>.

If the perfect tense (see pages 44–45) describes what has happened, the imperfect tense fills in information about what <u>was</u> <u>still</u> <u>happening</u> at the time:

• Ich <u>räumte</u> mein Schlafzimmer <u>auf</u>, als das Telefon geklingelt hat.
• I <u>was</u> <u>tidying</u> my room when the phone rang.

STRONG AND WEAK

*Weak t(ea), strong present(s): remember this and you'll find it easy to form the imperfect for these verbs, thus:

Weak/Regular (generally) insert the letter 't' into the present tense.

present tense	imperfect tense
ich spiele	ich spielte
du spielst	du spieltest
er/sie/es/man spielt	er/sie/es/man spielte, etc.

Strong/Irregular 'ich' and 'er/sie/es/man' are always the same; the other endings are the same as the present tense.

present tense	imperfect tense
ich sehe	ich sah
er/sie/es/man sieht	er/sie/es/man sah
du siehst	du sahst
wir sehen	wir sahen, etc

PART-TIME JOBS

babysitten	to baby sit
Ich trage Zeitungen aus	I deliver newspapers
Ich arbeite bei (WH Smith)	I work at (WH Smith)
Ich arbeite in einem Supermarkt/Restaurant/in einer Bäckerei	
I work in a supermarket/restaurant/baker's	
Ich bekomme/verdiene … Euros	
I get/earn … Euros	
pro Tag/Woche/Monat	per day/week/month
Ich kaufe/Ich spare mein Geld für CDs/Computerspiele/die Ferien	
I buy/I'm saving my money for CDs/computer games/holidays	

Maskulinum	Femininum	Neutrum
Babysitter (babysitter)	Arbeit (work)	Büro (office)
Kunde (customer)	Zeitung (newspaper)	Taxi(firma)
		taxi (company)
Teilzeitjob (part-time job)	Arbeitsstunde (hour's work)	

HOW TO FORM THE IMPERFECT TENSE

The imperfect tense is easy to form: for <u>regular/weak</u> verbs*, drop the -(e)n of the infinitive and add these endings:

singular	plural
ich + -<u>te</u>	wir + -<u>ten</u>
du + -<u>test</u>	ihr + -<u>tet</u>
er/sie/es/man + -<u>te</u>	sie + -<u>ten</u>

'you' singular and plural
Sie + -<u>ten</u>

e.g. How do you say 'I was doing …'?
mach<u>en</u> (infinitive 'to do')
drop -en ending
add -<u>te</u>: ich machte …

It is also easy to form for <u>irregular/strong</u> verbs*: once you have learnt by heart the imperfect <u>ich</u> form (see the box below) add these endings:

singular	plural
ich + -	wir + -en
du + -(e)st	ihr + -(e)t
er/sie/es/man + -	sie + -en

'you' singular and plural
Sie + -en

Infinitive	Imperfect 'Ich' form	Translation
denken	ich dachte	I thought/was thinking
essen	ich aß	I ate/was eating
fahren	ich fuhr	I travelled/was travelling
fliegen	ich flog	I flew/was flying
geben	ich gab	I gave/was giving
gehen	ich ging	I went/was going
haben	ich hatte	I had/was having
kommen	ich kam	I came/was coming
können	ich konnte	I could/was able to
müssen	ich musste	I had to/was having to
rufen	ich rief	I shouted/was shouting
schlagen	ich schlug	I beat/was beating
schreiben	ich schrieb	I wrote/was writing
sehen	ich sah	I saw/was seeing
sein	ich war	I was
singen	ich sang	I sang/was singing
stehen	ich stand	I stood/was standing
verstehen	ich verstand	I understood
wissen	ich wusste	I knew

e.g. How do you say 'You were sleeping?'?
schlafen (to sleep) → ich schlief
replace 'ich' with 'du'
add 'st': du schliefst

DESCRIPTIONS

ANGRIFF AUS MARS!!   MARTIAN ATTACK!!

Sie waren grün!
Das war an einem Samstagmorgen im Juni.
Es war halb zwölf.
Das Wetter war schön und es war ganz hell.
Ich war im Garten …
… als auf einmal eine fliegende Untertasse gelandet ist.
Es waren kleine grüne Marsbewohner überall.
Es war furchtbar! Ich hatte Angst!

They were green!
It was on a Saturday morning in June.
It was 11.30.
The weather was fine and it was quite a clear day.
I was in the garden …
… when suddenly a flying saucer landed.
There were little green Martians everywhere.
It was terrible! I was frightened!

You use the imperfect tense also to set the scene in the past: to say what time it was, what the weather was like, how you were feeling, etc., just as you do in English.

Note how there is often a time marker (als, auf einmal, dann, etc.) to provide a link between the perfect and imperfect tenses when you're describing events/setting the scene:
• Ich spielte, als sie gelandet sind.
• I was playing when they landed.

The third and final use of the imperfect tense is to translate 'used to', when you talk about doing the same things again and again in the past, e.g.:

• Jeden Tag in den Ferien stand ich um sechs Uhr auf.
• Every day during the holidays I used to get up at six o' clock.

The imperfect in German is used very much like the English (and less strictly than the perfect tense in French) to describe a series of fairly recent events:
• Zuerst ging ich in die Stadtmitte und kaufte mir ein Paar Schuhe. Dann traf ich mich mit meiner Freundin und wir gingen ins Kino.
• First I went into the town centre and bought myself a pair of shoes. Then I met my girlfriend and we went to the cinema.

PART-TIME JOBS AND WORK EXPERIENCE 1

WORK EXPERIENCE

Ich machte mein Arbeitspraktikum	I did my work experience
Ich arbeitete	I worked/was working/used to work
in einer Fabrik/bei einer Firma	in a factory/for a firm
in einem Büro	in an office
ich musste fotokopieren	I had to do the photocopying
Kunden anrufen/zurückrufen	phone/ring customers back
die Werkstatt aufräumen	tidy the workshop
Akten organisieren	organise files/documents
Ich half dem Chef	I used to help the boss
Ich schrieb (Kunden)briefe	I used to write letters (to customers)
Ich musste jeden Tag den Bus/Zug/die Straßenbahn nehmen	I had to take the bus/train/ tram every day
Als Lohn verdiente ich zwei Euros die (Arbeits)stunde	My pay was two Euros an hour

AM TELEFON

FORMELLE ANRUFE/ FORMAL BUSINESS CALLS

A — *Hallo? Bertelsmann*
Hello? Bertelsmann's

→ **B** — *Hallo, hier ist Frau Braun.Kann ich bitte Herrn Schmidt sprechen*
Hello, Frau Braun speaking. May I speak to Mr. Schmidt?

A — *Ja, einen Moment, bitte. Ich verbinde Sie.*
Yes, one moment please. I'll put you through.

A — *Nein, er ist leider im Moment nicht hier. Soll ich etwas ausrichten?*
No, I'm afraid he's not here at the moment. Can I take a message?

A — *Es tut mir leid, er spricht gerade.Wollen Sie warten oder wollen Sie es später wieder versuchen?*
I'm sorry, his line's busy. Would you like to hold or try again later?

B — *Gut, danke.*
Good, thank you.

B — *Ja, bitte. Sagen Sie ihm, dass* Frau Braun angerufen hat.*
Yes, please. Tell him Mrs Braun called.

B — *Danke, ich warte/ Nein, danke. Ich rufe morgen wieder an.*
Thanks, I'll hold./No, thanks. I'll call back tomorrow.

A — *Gerne/danke. Auf wiederhören.*
Of course/thank you. Goodbye.

B — *Auf Wiederhören.*
Goodbye.

PERSÖNLICHE ANRUFE/ PERSONAL/PRIVATE CALLS

A — *Schätzle?*
(Mr/Mrs/Ms)Schätzle speaking

→ **B** — *Hallo, hier ist Christa. Ist Markus da?*
Hello, this is Christa. Is Markus there?

A — *Ja, (einen) Moment mal. Ich hole ihn.*
Yes, just a moment. I'll fetch him.

B — *Leider nicht. Soll ich etwas ausrichten, oder möchtest du es später noch einmal versuchen?*
Afraid not. Can I take a message, or do you want to try again later?

A — *Gut, danke.*
Good, thanks.

A — *Ja, bitte. Sagen Sie ihm, dass* Christa angerufen hat/Nein, danke. Ich rufe später wieder an.*
Yes, please. Tell him Christa called./No, thanks, I'll try again later.

Examiner's Top Tip

*As you'll need to leave a message at some point , remember that 'dass' is a subordinating conjunction, so the verb goes to the end (see pages 76–77). Show off your knowledge, using modals like 'können', 'müssen', 'sollen' and 'dürfen': Sagen Sie ihr, dass ich heute abend leider nicht zum Konzert gehen kann/darf. Tell her that unfortunately I can't/I'm not allowed to go to the concert this evening.

PART-TIME JOBS AND WORK EXPERIENCE 2

EHRLICH?!

ANGRIFF AUS MARS! (TEIL 2) MARTIAN ATTACK! (PART 2)

Ich zitterte vor Furcht hinter einem Baum. Die Marsbewohner sind aus der fliegenden Untertasse herausgestiegen. Dann bildeten sie einen Kreis und redeten miteinander. An diesem Moment miaute meine Katze ganz laut. 'Leise, Mietze!' flüsterte ich. Das war leider zu spät. Einer der Marsbewohner kam auf meinen Baum zu.
Mit pochendem Herz sah ich, dass auch die anderen Marsbewohner in meiner Richtung blickten.
Plötzlich blieb der kleine Marsbewohner stehen und hörte aufmerksam zu. Warum denn? Ich wusste nicht warum. Dann wurde es mir klar. Jemand sang! Das war mein Bruder, der sich duschte!

I was trembling with fear behind a tree. The Martians got out of the flying saucer. Then they got into a circle and talked to one another. At that moment my cat miaowed loudly. 'Shh! Puss!' I whispered. But it was too late. One of the Martians was approaching my tree.
With a pounding heart I saw that the other Martians were also looking in my direction. Suddenly the little Martian stopped and listened attentively. Why?
I didn't know. Then I understood. Somebody was singing! It was my brother who was in the shower!

The Imperfect and Perfect Tenses

You can use the imperfect and perfect tenses to talk about films and books you've seen and read. Here are some useful expressions to help you:

es handelt sich um (+ accusative)
it's about
einen Jungen und seine Familie
a boy and his family
es gibt/sind fünf (handelnde) Personen
there are five characters/people
der Film/das Buch hat mir gut/gar nicht gefallen
I liked/didn't like at all the film/book
es war ganz spannend/langweilig
it was exciting/boring

QUICK TEST

Say/write it in English:

1. Es war Viertel nach elf.

2. Was machten sie?

3. Wir waren auf Urlaub.

4. Es regnete und war furchtbar kalt.

Say/write it in German:

5. I was cooking.

6. You used to deliver newspapers.

7. What time was it?

8. I was sleeping when you went home.

9. There were three characters in the film.

10. Suddenly I saw that my parents were there.

Examiner's Top Tip
Remember: in a story or a report of an event, you can probably work in three tenses: the perfect and imperfect for the events in the past, and the present tense for direct speech.

1. It was 11.15.
2. What were they doing?
3. We were on holiday.
4. It was raining and was terribly cold.
5. Ich kochte.
6. Du trugst Zeitungen aus.
7. Wie spät/Wie viel Uhr war es?
8. Ich schlief (war eingeschlafen), als du nach Hause gegangen bist.
9. Es waren/gab drei Personen im Film.
10. Plötzlich/auf einmal sah ich, dass mein Eltern da waren.

LEISURE ①

DIRECT OBJECT PRONOUNS

There's no need to be frightened of 'cases' in German. Get your teeth into these:

SUBJECTS AND SUBJECT PRONOUNS: THE NOMINATIVE CASE

The subject of a sentence – also known in German as the Nominative (or naming) case – names the doer of the verb:

Nadia hat den Horrorfilm schon gesehen.
Nadia has already seen the horror film.

'Nadia' is the subject (or the name of the person) who has seen the film. Another word for 'name' is 'noun'. If you shorten this noun to 'she', you make it into a subject pronoun:

Sie hat den Horrorfilm schon gesehen.
She has already seen the horror film.

Now sie (she) is the subject of the sentence. Look at these sentences and work out why the underlined words are the subject or subject pronouns of their sentences:

Markus lädt mich zum Kino ein.
Markus is inviting me to the cinema.

Er lädt mich zum Kino ein.
He is inviting me to the cinema.

Morgen besuchen meine Eltern und ich den Freizeitpark.
Tomorrow my parents and I are going to visit the leisure park.

Morgen besuchen wir den Freizeitpark.
Tomorrow we are going to visit the leisure park

Answer:
Markus/he is the one who is doing the inviting. My parents and I/we are the ones doing the visiting: so these are the subjects/subject pronouns.

DIRECT OBJECTS AND DIRECT OBJECT PRONOUNS: THE ACCUSATIVE CASE

The direct object, also known in German as the Accusative (or named/accused) case, tells you who or what suffered at the hands of the subject. In the example above, ask yourself 'whom' or 'what' has Nadia already seen – answer, the 'horror film', so it is in the Accusative case:

Nadia hat den Horrorfilm schon gesehen.
Nadia has already seen the horror film.

Just as you can have subject pronouns, you can also have direct object pronouns:

Nadia hat ihn schon gesehen.
Nadia has already seen it.

Now look at these sentences and work out why the underlined words are the direct object or direct object pronouns of their sentences:

Markus lädt Nadia zum Kino ein.
Markus is inviting Nadia to the cinema.

Er lädt sie zum Kino ein.
He is inviting her to the cinema.

Morgen besuchen meine Eltern und ich den Freizeitpark.
Tomorrow my parents and I are going to visit the leisure park.

Wir besuchen ihn morgen.
We're going to visit it tomorrow.

Answers:
Nadia/her is being invited; den Freizeitpark/ihn is being visited: so these are the direct objects/direct object pronouns.

Learn this table by heart and you'll find direct object pronouns easy to digest

Subject	Direct Object Pronoun	Translation
Ich	mich	me
du	dich	you (singular)
er*	ihn	him/it (masculine nouns)
sie*	sie	she/it (feminine nouns)
es*	es	it (neuter nouns)
wir	uns	us
ihr	euch	you (plural)
Sie	Sie	you (singular & plural)
sie*	sie	them

Examiner's Top Tip

This list deals with personal pronouns, such as 'I', 'you', etc., but remember that you can replace any noun with a pronoun, following this pattern:

Nominative	Nom pronoun	Acc pronoun
der -	er*(he/it)	ihn (him/it)
die	sie*(she/it)	sie (she/it)
das	es*(it)	es (it)
die	sie*(they)	sie (them)

Using these pronouns will definitely improve your German.

GET OUT AND ABOUT

Was gibt es hier für Jugendliche?
What is there here for young people?

Eigentlich gar nichts/nicht viel.
Actually nothing at all/not much.

Es gibt jede Menge zu tun.
There's loads to do.

Es gibt den Freizeitpark.
There's the leisure park.
Konzerte in der Stadthalle.
Concerts in the municipal hall.

Sportplätze.
Sports grounds.

Theaterstücke und Filmvereine.
Plays and film societies.

Maskulinum (der)
Abenteuerfilm
adventure film
Dokumentarfilm
a documentary
Horrorfilm
a horror film
Krimi
a thriller
Liebesfilm
a love story
Lustfilm
a comedy
Science-fictionfilm
a science fiction film
Untertitel
subtitle
Zirkus
circus

Femininum (die)
Anzeige
advertisement, display board
Einladung
invitation
Karte
card, ticket
Nachrichten (plural)
news
Sendung
broadcast, programme (T.V./radio)
Serie
series, serial
Überraschung
surprise
Versammlung
meeting
Vorstellung
show, performance

Neutrum (das)
Eintrittsgeld
cost, money to get in
Informationsbüro
information office
Kino
cinema
Konzert
concert
Programm
programme
Sportzentrum
sports centre
Theaterstück
play

HOME OR AWAY?

·Ich gehe heute Abend (nicht) aus.
I'm (not) going out this evening.
·Ich bleibe lieber** zu Hause.
I'd rather stay at home.
·Kommst du zu mir?
Do you want to come to my house?
·Sehen wir fern?
Shall we watch TV?
·Was für ein (Fernseh)film ist das?
What sort of (TV) film is it?

Ich warte auf dich
I'll wait for you
Warte auf mich
Wait for me
Am Hauptbahnhof
outside the main station
in der Hauptstraße
in the High Street
im Stadion
inside the stadium
am Eingang
near the entrance
vor der Kirche
in front of the church
gegenüber dem Museum

Examiner's Top Tip
**Don't forget to use 'lieber' and 'am liebsten' to tell people what you prefer or like best:
Ich sehe lieber Horrorfilme.
Ich finde sie toll!
I prefer watching horror films
I think they're great!
Am liebsten aber gehe ich zum Sportzentrum.
But best of all I like going to the sports centre.

Examiner's Top Tip
Remember to take the chance to show off your knowledge of prepositions (see pages 16–17 and 30–31) by giving times (um, gegen) and places where people arrange to meet (an, auf, gegenüber, hinter, in, neben, über, unter, vor, zwischen). Remember also that you'll probably be using the dative case because you will be talking about fixed places/positions (see pages 30–31).

Kommst du mit?
Are you coming along?
Was schlägst du vor?
What do you suggest?
Lädst du mich ein?
Are you inviting me (out)?
Gehen wir ins Kino/Theater/zum Konzert/Zirkus?
Shall we go to the cinema/theatre/concert/circus?

Was läuft? — What's on/showing?
Wann und wo treffen wir uns? — When and where shall we meet?
Um/gegen (halb) acht — at/about eight (seven thirty)
Um Viertel nach sechs/vor neun — at 6.15/8.45

INTERVIEW

Was gibt es hier in der Stadt zu tun? Sind Sie damit zufrieden?
What is there to do in this town? Are you satisfied with what there is?

Nein, überhaupt nicht. Es gibt doch viel zu tun, aber nicht für junge Leute.
No, not all (satisfied). There is lots to do but not for young people.

Wieso denn? Ist das alles nur für ältere Leute gemeint?
How come? Is it all only meant for older people?

Na, wenn man sich für Bibliotheken, Museen und Theaters interessiert, kann man sagen, dass es hier ganz cool ist, aber …
Well, if you're interested in libraries, museums and theatres, then it's fair to say that it's really cool here, but …

Gibt es doch keine Sportangelegenheiten?
Aren't there any sporting opportunities?

Doch, aber das interessiert mich nicht so sehr. Ich finde es langweilig und viel zu anstrengend.
Well yes, but I'm not that interested. I think it's boring and much too energetic.

Gibt es denn keine Cafés, Discos und Jugendklubs?
So, aren't there any cafes, discos and youth clubs?

Die meisten Cafés sind voller Touristen und alte Leute. Und die beste Disko in der Stadtmitte schließt um halb elf.
Most of the cafes are full of tourists and old people. And the best disco in the town centre shuts at 10.30 p.m.

Und die Jugendklubs?
And the youth clubs?

Ach was, das ist nichts für mich. Ich finde sie blöd. Ich bleibe lieber zu Hause und sehe fern.
Oh, that's not the kind of thing I like. I think they're stupid. I'd rather stay at home and watch TV.

FUßBALLFANATIKER

Ich spiele seit* zehn Jahren Fußball und ich bin seit drei Jahren Mitglied der Schulmannschaft. Wir trainieren und spielen hart und die meisten Mitspieler sind topfit. Es freut mich besonders, dass wir so viel geleistet haben. Wir haben zwar viele Spiele gewonnen und haben letztes Jahr auch das Pokal gewonnen, aber das ist nicht am wichtigsten: wir sind alle auch gute Freunde und unternehmen immer etwas zusammen nach dem Spiel. Das macht riesigen Spaß!

I have been playing football for ten years and have been a member of the school team for three years. We train and play hard and most of the players are really fit. I'm really pleased that we've been so successful. In fact, we've won lots of our games and we also won the cup last year, but that's not the most important thing: we're all good friends and we always do something together after matches. It's terrific fun!

Examiner's Top Tip
Don't be afraid to include the occasional, doch, überhaupt (nich denn and ach was in your expre sion of opinions on what there i do and see in your area. Remer too, to use intonation to empha some of your points.

WAS LÄUFT?

Was machen wir denn am Wochenede?
What shall we do this weekend?

Ich weiß nicht. Hast du Lust, schwimmen zu gehen?
I don't know. Do you fancy going swimming?

Nein, ich habe keine Lust. Was machen wir sonst?
No, I don't fancy that. What else can we do?

Willst du zum Theater oder ins Kino gehen?
Do you want to go to the theatre or the cinema?

Null Bock aufs Theater. Was läuft im Moment im Kino?
Theatre – no chance! What's on at the cinema at the moment?

'Blutfest' – ein Horrorfilm mit Boris Blutsauger.
'Bloodbath' a horror film with Boris Bloodsucker.

Ach, schade, ich hab' es schon gesehen. Das ist ein toller Film!
Oh, that's a shame, I've already seen it. It's a great film!

Gehen wir zum Freizeitpark? Ich warte auf dich um halb sechs im Eiscafé.
Shall we go to the leisure park? I'll wait for you at 5.30 in the ice cream parlour.

LEISURE 2

QUICK TEST

Say/write it in English:

1. Es gibt nichts zu tun.

2. Ich finde es langweilig.

3. Warte auf ihn dort drüben.

4. Ich wohne seit drei Monaten hier.

Say/write it in German:

5. We'd rather go swimming.

6. There's the leisure park and the sports centre.

7. Do you fancy going to the pop concert in the stadium this evening?

8. They have been playing hockey for nine months.

9. Does he want to watch TV at 6.30?

10. The plays? I've already seen them.

tenses

*When you want to say that you have been doing something for some time, you use seit with the present tense, because you are still doing it:
Ich wohne seit fünf Jahren hier.
I have lived (and am still living) here for five years.
Similarly, if you want to say that you had been doing something for some time, you use seit with the imperfect tense, because at that time you were still doing it:
Ich spielte seit zwei Jahren Tennis.
I had been playing tennis for two years

1. There's nothing to do.
2. I find it boring.
3. Wait for him over there.
4. I've lived here for three months.
5. Wir gehen lieber schwimmen.
6. Es gibt den Freizeitpark und das Sportzentrum.
7. Hast du/Haben Sie/Habt ihr Lust, heute Abend zum Popkonzert im Stadion zu gehen?
8. Sie spielen seit neun Monaten Hockey.
9. Will er um halb sieben fernsehen?
10. Die Theaterstücke? Ich habe sie schon gesehen.

THIS, THAT AND THE OTHER

To say 'this', you use <u>dieser</u>.
To say 'that', you use <u>jener</u>.
Dieser and jener must <u>agree</u> with the noun they refer to.
Their endings change according to:
a) the <u>gender</u> of the noun – or whether the noun is <u>plural</u>.
b) the <u>case</u> that the noun is in.

Here is a table, showing <u>dieser</u> and <u>jener</u> in all three cases:

	Masculine	Feminine	Neuter	Plural
Nominative	dieser/jener	diese/jene	dieses/jenes	diese/jene
Accusative	diesen/jenen	diese/jene	dieses/jenes	diese/jene
Dative	diesem/jenem	dieser/jener	diesem/jenem	diesen/jenen

If you want to just say 'this one/these ones' or 'that one/those ones':
Put a capital letter at the beginning of dieser or jener.
Make sure the ending is right (according to gender and case, as above).
e.g.
Welches Hemd kaufen Sie?
Which shirt are you buying?
Ich nehme <u>Dieses</u> hier.
I'll take this one.

NB .When you are shopping for clothes, you use mostly the nominative and accusative cases:

Masculine Noun
Nominative Case
Die<u>ser</u> Pullover ist schön.
This jumper's nice.

Masculine Noun
Accusative Case
Ich nehme die<u>sen</u> Pullover.
I'll take this jumper.

Feminine Noun
Nominative Case
Jene Jeans gefällt mir.
I like those jeans.

Feminine Noun
Accusative Case
Ich möchte jen<u>e</u> Jeans anprobieren.
I'd like to try on those jeans.

AT THE CLOTHES SHOP

MASKULINUM (DER)

Badeanzug	swimming costume
Hut	hat
Mantel	coat
Regenmantel	raincoat
Pulli (Pullover)	jumper
Pyjama	
Schlafanzug	pyjamas
Regenschirm	umbrella
Rock	skirt
Schal	scarf
Schlips	tie
(NB also: die Krawatte)	
Trainingsanzug	tracksuit

FEMININUM (DIE)

Badehose	swimming trunks
Baseballmütze	baseball cap
Bluse	blouse
Hose	trousers
Jacke	jacket
Jeans	jeans
Krawatte	tie
(NB. also: der Schlips)	
Shorts	shorts
Sonnenbrille	sunglasses

NEUTRUM (DAS)

Hemd	shirt
Kleid	dress
Sweatshirt	sweatshirt
T-Shirt	tee shirt

PLURAL (DIE)

Handschuhe	gloves
Schuhe	shoes
Socken	socks
Turnschuhe	trainers

Instead of repeating the name of a piece of clothing you want to buy, you can use the word for 'it' or 'them'. This will help to show the examiner what you can do! Remember, there are three genders in German, so there are three words for 'it'. In the accusative case (direct object pronouns), they are:
Masculine: ihn
Feminine: sie
Neuter: es
The word for 'them' is sie
e.g.
Ich nehme diesen Rock
I'll take this skirt
Ich nehme ihn
I'll take it
Möchten Sie jene Shorts anprobieren?
Would you like to try those shorts on?
Möchten Sie sie anprobieren?
Would you like to try them (it) on?

ADJECTIVES WITH 'ZU' & 'GENUG'

To say something is too big, small, expensive, etc., you use <u>zu</u>:
Es ist zu groß. It's too big.
You can also say:
Es ist mir zu groß. It's too big (for me)
To say something is not big, long (etc.) enough, you use <u>nicht</u> ... <u>genug</u>:
Sie ist nicht groß genug. It's not big enough.

Masculine	Er ist		groß (big)
Feminine	Sie ist	(mir) zu	klein (small)
Neuter	Es ist		lang (long)
Plural	Sie sind		kurz (short)
			teuer (expensive)

SHOPPING 1

AT THE MARKET

OBST UND GEMÜSE

...ININUM

...elsine(n) }	orange(s)
...nge(n) }	
...nane(n)	banana(s)
...hne(n)	bean(s)
...beere(n)	strawberry(ies)
...mbeere(n)	raspberry(ies)
...rotte(n) }	carrots
...öhre(n) }	
...rtoffel(n)	potato(es)
...rsche(n)	cherry(ies)
...elone(n)	melon(s)
...ampelmuse(n) }	grapefruit
...rapefruit(-) }	
...flaume(n)	plum(s)
...omate(n)	tomatoes
...itrone(n)	lemon(s)
...wiebel(n)	onion(s)

MASKULINUM

Apfel (Äpfel)	apple(s)
Knoblauch	garlic
Pfirsich(e)	peach(es)
Pilz(e) }	mushroom(s)
Champignon(s) }	

Ich möchte ... }	I'd like ...
Ich hätte gern ...	
Ich brauche ...	I need
Geben Sie mir bitte ...	Please can I have...
Haben Sie ...?	Have you got...?
500 Gramm ... }	500 grammes of..
ein Pfund ...	
ein Kilo ...	a kilo of ...
ein(e) ...	a/an ...
etwas ...	some ...
Was kostet das?	How much is that?
Was kostet...	How much is it
... das Stück?	... a piece / each?
... das Kilo?	... a kilo?
Ich nehme...	I'll take ...
Sonst noch etwas?	Anything else?
Das wäre alles	That's all

Examiner's Top Tip

When shopping for fruit and vegetables, it will be mostly the plural version of the noun you need, but it's worth knowing the singular and gender of the bigger fruits, in case you want to ask for just one. With most other items of food and drink, it's usually the singular you need.

AT THE SUPERMARKET

zwei Stück Torte/Kuchen	two pieces of gâteau/cake
ein Paket Müsli/Nudeln	a packet of muesli/pasta
eine Packung Kekse/Chips	a packet of biscuits/crisps
vier Scheiben Schinken	four slices of ham
eine Dose Tomaten	a tin/can of tomatoes
eine Flasche Mineralwasser	a bottle of mineral water
eine Tüte Bonbons	a bag of sweets
vier Tüten Nüsse	four bags of nuts
eine Schachtel Pralinen	a box of chocolates
eine Tafel Schokolade	a bar of chocolate

MASKULINUM

Apfelsaft	apple juice
Orangensaft	orange juice
Käse	cheese
Honig	honey
Zucker	sugar

FEMININUM

Bockwurst	cold sausage
Bratwurst	sausages for frying
Limonade	lemonade
Milch	milk
Salami	salami
Schwarzwälderkirschtorte	Black Forest gâteau

NEUTRUM

Brot	bread
Kaugummi	chewing gum
Ei(er)	egg(s)
Hähnchen	chicken

SHOPS

MASKULINUM (DER/EIN)

Laden (Läden)	shop(s)
Markt	market
Supermarkt	supermarket
Tabakwaren	tobacconist's
Verbrauchermarkt	hypermarket

FEMININUM (DIE/EINE)

Apotheke	chemist
Bäckerei	baker's
Buchhandlung	bookshop
Drogerie	drugstore
Konditorei	cake shop
Metzgerei	butcher's

NEUTRUM (DAS/EIN)

Einkaufszentrum	shopping centre
Geschäft(e)	shop(s)
Kaufhaus	department store
Lebensmittelgeschäft	general store/grocer's
Süßwarengeschäft	sweet shop

AM MARKT

Guten Tag. Was möchten Sie, bitte?
Hello. What would you like, please?

Ich hätte gern ein Kilo Äpfel, bitte.
I'd like a kilo of apples, please.

Sonst noch etwas?
Anything else?

Haben Sie bitte Kirschen?
Do you have any cherries, please?

Sicher. Sie sind hier.
Of course. They're here.

Gut, na, geben Sie mir 500 Gramm, bitte.
Right, can I have 500 grammes, please.

Ich brauche auch Pfirsiche.
I need peaches, too

Es tut mir leid, ich habe keine Pfirsiche.
I'm sorry, I haven't got any peaches.

Macht nichts. Ich nehme ein Pfund Bohnen, bitte.
Never mind. I'll take 500 grammes of beans, please.

Danke. Das macht drei Euros fünfzig, bitte.
Thank you. That comes to three Euros 50, please.

IM SUPERMARKT

Karl, wir brauchen 200 Gramm Käse und fünf oder sechs Scheiben Bockwurst. Karl, we need 200 grammes of cheese and five or six slices of sausage.

Ist das alles? Brauchen wir auch Schinken?
Is that all? Do we need ham, too?

Nein, Schinken haben wir. Aber du kannst bitte eine Dose Frankfurter nehmen.
No, we've got ham. But you can get a tin of Frankfurters, please.

Oh, und zwei Tüten Milch, auch.
Oh, and two packs of milk, too.

Also. Was gibt's noch auf meiner Liste?
Right, what else is on my list?

Sprudel – eine Flasche.... Kuchen oder Torte – das kaufen wir am besten in der Konditorei ... eine große Packung Chips für das Picknick....
Mineral water – a bottle ... cake or gâteau – we'd better buy that in the cake shop ... a big packet of crisps for the picnic....

Bitte, Mutti. Und die Eier? Wo sind die Eier?
There you are, Mum. What about the eggs? Where are the eggs?

Die kaufen wir im Lebensmittelgeschäft – dort sind sie organisch und immer frisch.
We'll buy those in the grocer's – they're organic there and always fresh.

EINKAUFEN GEHEN

•Gehst du gern einkaufen? Wohin gehst du, wie oft und mit wem?
Do you like going shopping? Where do you go, how often and with whom?

•Ja, samstags machen meine Freunde und ich oft einen Einkaufsbummel. Normalerweise fahren wir mit dem Bus zum Einkaufszentrum....
Yes, on Saturdays my mates and I often go on a shopping trip. Usually we take the bus to the shopping centre....

•Dort gibt es allerlei Läden – Kleidungsgeschäfte, ein großes Kaufhaus, wo man alles finden kann....
In there there are all sorts of shops – clothes shops, a big department store, where you can find anything.

•Ich gehe lieber ins Einkaufzentrum, weil es so praktisch ist und wenn es regnet, bleibt man immer trocken!
I prefer going to the shopping centre, because it's so convenient and if it rains, you stay dry!

SHOPPING 2

KLEIDER KAUFEN

GESCHLOSSEN (Closed)

• Entschuldigung. Wo ist die Damenabteilung/Herrenabteilung, bitte?
Excuse me. Where is the women's/men's department, please?

• Sie ist im dritten Stock. Nehmen Sie die Rolltreppe, dort drüben.
It's on the third floor. Take the escalator, over there.

• Kann ich Ihnen helfen?
Can I help you?

• Ich suche einen blauen oder einen schwarzen Pulli, bitte.
I'm looking for a blue or black jumper, please.

• Wir haben zwei Sorten. Diese hier sind aus Baumwolle, jene da sind aus Wolle.
We've got two sorts. These ones are made of cotton. Those ones are made of wool.

• Dieser hier gefällt mir. Darf ich ihn bitte anprobieren?
I like this one. Can I try it on, please?

• Natürlich. Welche Größe?
Of course. What size?

• Mittelgroß, bitte.
Medium, please.

• Die Anprobekabinen sind hinten, rechts.
The fitting rooms are at the back, on the right.

• Vielen Dank.
Thank you very much.

GEÖFFNET (Open)

SONDERANGEBOT (Sale)

• Passt er Ihnen?
Is it all right?

• Er ist mir zu klein. Haben Sie etwas Größeres?
It's too small for me. Do you have anything bigger?

• Es tut mir leid. Die sind alle.
I'm sorry. We haven't got any more.

• Ich nehme ihn. Akzeptieren Sie Reiseschecks?
I'll take it. Do you accept traveller's cheques?

• Ich möchte mich beschweren. Ich habe diesen Pulli hier gestern gekauft und es gibt ein Loch darin.
I'd like to complain. I bought this jumper here yesterday and there's a hole in it.

• Es tut mir leid. Möchten Sie einen anderen?
I'm sorry. Would you like another one?

• Nein, danke. Ich möchte eine Rückzahlung.
No thank you. I'd like a refund.

Examiner's Top Tip
Use 'gefallen' + the dative to say you like something:
Er (der Pulli) gefällt mir.
I like it (the jumper).
You can also use the dative to say something fits/suits someone – with the verb 'passen':
Er passt mir nicht gut, aber er passt dir sehr gut!
It doesn't suit me, but it suits you very well!

Notice how you say 'something bigger' – <u>etwas Größeres</u>. To say 'bigger', 'smaller', 'cheaper', etc. you just add -'er' to the adjective. This is called the comparative (see page 58). With '<u>groß</u>', you also add an umlaut to the 'o' – <u>größer</u> (bigger).
If you want to say 'something big/bigger, small/smaller' etc., you use '<u>etwas</u>' (something), put a capital letter on the front of the adjective and add -'es' to the end of the adjective:

<u>klein</u>	(small)
<u>etwas Kleines</u>	(something small)
<u>kleiner</u>	(smaller)
<u>etwas Kleineres</u>	(something smaller)

QUICK TEST

Say/write it in English:
1. Diese Woche: Sonderangebot.
2. Welche Größe sind Sie?
3. Leider habe ich keine Himbeeren mehr.
4. Im Lebensmittelgeschäft muss ich Kirschen kaufen.

Say/write it in German:
5. I'm looking for a white shirt, please.
6. May I try this shirt on, please?
7. I'll take that shirt, please.
8. I'd like a bottle of apple juice and a bar of chocolate, please.
9. I go on a shopping trip every weekend.
10. I'd like to complain.

10. Ich möchte mich beschweren.
9. Ich mache jedes Wochenende einen Einkaufsbummel.
8. Ich möchte/hätte gern eine Flasche Apfelsaft und eine Tafel Schokolade, bitte.
7. Ich nehme jenes Hemd, bitte.
6. Darf ich bitte dieses Hemd anprobieren?
5. Ich suche ein weißes Hemd, bitte.
4. I must buy some cherries in the grocer's/general store.
3. Unfortunately, I haven't any raspberries left.
2. What size do you take?
1. This week: sale/special offer

Speaking

Role Play 1
You are at a market in Germany:
• Ask for 500 grammes of mushrooms. (1 mark)
• Ask whether they have any strawberries. (1 mark)
• Say you will take a kilo of pears. (1 mark)
• Ask how much it is. (1 mark)

(4 marks)

Role Play 2
You are shopping for clothes in Germany:
• Say that you are looking for a pair of trousers. (1 mark)
• Say you like these ones. (1 mark)
• Ask whether you can try them on. (1 mark)
• Say they are too big for you. (1 mark)

(4 marks)

General Conversation

1. Wie hilfst du deinen Eltern zu Hause? (1 mark)
2. Wie hast du ihnen letztes Wochenende geholfen? (1 mark)
3. Mittags isst man meistens kalt oder heiß bei dir? (1 mark)
4. Was hast du heute zum Frühstück gegessen? (Choose one) (1 mark)
5. Kannst du mir dein Lieblingsgericht beschreiben? (1 mark)
6. Isst du meistens gesund? (1 mark)
7. Was machst du sonst, um fit zu bleiben? (1 mark)
8. Hast du einen Teilzeitjob? (1 mark)
9. Sag mir etwas über dein Arbeitspraktikum. (1 mark)
10. Was gibt es in deiner Gegend für Jugendliche und bist du damit zufrieden? (1 mark)
11. Beschreib einen Film, den du neulich gesehen hast. (1 mark)
12. Kannst du mir deinen letzten Einkaufsbummel beschreiben? (1 mark)

(12 marks)

Writing

1. You have received an email from your German friend, Eva. She wants to know about your pocket money, whether you have a part-time job and what your work experience was like.
    Schreib einen Brief auf Deutsch. Beantworte folgende Fragen:
    • Bekommst du Taschengeld? (1 mark)
    • Hast du einen Teilzeitjob? (1 mark)
    • Wie findest du ihn? (1 mark)
    • Wo hast du dein Arbeitspraktikum gemacht? (2 marks)
    • Was musstest du machen? (2 marks)
    • Hat es dir gefallen? (1 mark)
    • Warum? (1 mark)
    • Stell Eva eine Frage über ihren Job. (1 mark)

(10 marks)

2. Du hast einen Artikel über die Faschingszeit in einer deutschen Zeitschrift gelesen. Schreib einen Artikel über Feste bei dir.
    Beantworte folgende Fragen:
    • Welches ist das wichtigste Fest für dich? (1 mark)
    • Wie findest du dieses Fest? Warum? (2 marks)
    • Wie feiert man es bei dir? (1 mark)
    • Isst man oder trinkt man etwas Besonderes? (1 mark)
    • Wie hast du deinen letzten Geburtstag gefeiert? (2 marks)
    • Was hast du bekommen? (1 mark)
    • Wie möchtest du deinen nächsten Geburtstag feiern? (2 mark)

(10 marks)

Reading

1. Lies folgenden Text:

> **Vom ersten Oktober: SONDERANGEBOT**
> **In der Herrenabteilung: Mäntel und**
> **Jacken aus Leder**
> **In der Damenabteilung: Hemden, Kleider und Schale**
> **aus Baumwolle oder Wolle.**
> **Im dritten Stock: alles für Sportliche!**
> **Wir akzeptieren Kreditkarten und Reiseschecks!**

Schreib R (Richtig) oder F (Falsch):
1. Das Sonderangebot ist im Herbst. (1 mark)
2. Man kann Männerhemden aus Baumwolle im Sonderangebot kaufen. (1 mark)
3. Die Turnschuhe und Trainingsanzüge sind im dritten Stock. (1 mark)
4. Es gibt Lederschuhe für Männer im Sonderangebot. (1 mark)
5. Man darf nicht mit Reiseschecks zahlen. (1 mark)

(5 marks)

2. Lies folgenden Text:

Was muss man tun, um fit zu ⬚1⬚? Du weißt, du sollst ⬚2⬚ Fettiges essen, du sollst ⬚3⬚ rauchen und keinen ⬚4⬚ trinken. Aber weißt du, dass die Hausarbeit fit macht?! Letzten Samstag hast du deinen Eltern im Haus oder im Garten ⬚5⬚? Vielleicht hast du dein Zimmer ⬚6⬚, dein ⬚7⬚ gemacht, oder Staub gesaugt? Bei solchen Aktivitäten kann man fitter und ⬚8⬚ werden. Aber am Besten machst du die Gartenarbeit: wenn du den ⬚9⬚ mähst, bist du oft aktiver als beim Training!

Schreib die passenden Buchstaben.
Bespiel: 1D

A. Alkohol	E. eingekauft	I. nicht
B. aufgeräumt	F. geholfen	J. nichts
C. Bett	G. gesunder	K. Rasen
D. bleiben	H. größer	

(8 marks)

3. Lies folgenden Text:

> **Wir hatten euch gefragt: Was war euer bester Teilzeitjob? Und der Schlimmste? Oder der Ungewöhnlichste? Diese Woche schickte uns Dieter Müller aus Freiburg diese E-Mail:**
>
> Vor drei Jahren bekam ich einen Nebenjob in einem Haustiergeschäft. Ich musste jeden Samstag von Viertel vor neun bis halb sechs arbeiten und verdiente drei Euros die Stunde. Die Arbeit fand ich unterschiedlich und interessant, aber ganz anstregend! Erst morgens sollte ich alle Tiere füttern. Das heißt erstens das Futter vorbereiten: Obst für die Vögel aufschneiden und mit Nüssen und Körnern mischen. Grüngemüse für die Meerschweinchen vorbereitete ich auch. Die Hunde und Katzen waren ziemlich leichter: ich eröffnete die Dosen und steckte ihnen das Fleisch auf den Teller. Glücklicherweise bin ich kein Vegetarier! Die Tiere waren meistens sehr süß – nur einmal biss mir die Hand ein böses Kaninchen! – und ich hatte Angst nur vor einem: Schlangen kann ich nicht leiden und im Laden hatten wir drei, deren ich den Käfig jede Woche sauber machen musste. Jeden Samstag war ich schließlich total erschöpft aber ganz zufrieden, weil ich Tiere so gern habe. Ich habe mich vielleicht vor, Tierarzt zu werden.

Beantworte folgenden Fragen auf Deutsch:
a) Gefiel Dieter sein Teilzeitberuf? (1 mark)
b) Warum (nicht)? (1 mark)
c) Welche Tiere aßen Äpfel, Bananen, und so weiter? (1 mark)
d) Welchen Tieren musste Dieter Gemüse geben? (1 mark)
e) Welches Tier hat ihn verletzt? (1 mark)
f) Vor welchem Tier hatte er Angst? (1 mark)
g) Welchen Beruf möchte Dieter in die Zukunft wählen? (1 mark)

(7 marks)

How did you do?

1–20	correct	start again
21–35	correct	getting there
36–49	correct	good work
50–60	correct	excellent

CHARACTER AND PERSONAL RELATIONSHIPS 1

CONJUNCTIONS

A conjunction is a simple word that is used to join other words together, to form lists or make longer sentences. In German, there are two kinds of conjunction: <u>co-ordinating conjunctions</u> and <u>subordinating conjunctions</u>.

CO-ORDINATING CONJUNCTIONS

The conjunctions: <u>und</u> (and), <u>aber</u> (but), <u>oder</u> (or), <u>sondern</u> (but – after a negative), <u>denn</u> (because) are so easy to use that they are almost invisible: you don't need to do anything to the word order, just slip them in and hook up as many words and parts of sentences as you like. For example, you could make these six sentences into one, simply by using the conjunctions listed above:

Mein bester Freund ist nicht launisch. My best friend isn't moody.	Er ist witzig. He's witty.	Er ist immer hilfsbereit He's always helpful	Er ist mitfühlend. He's sympathetic.	Er ist nie neidisch. He's never jealous.	Er ist selbstsicher. He's confident/sure of himself.

Mein bester Freund ist nicht launisch <u>sondern</u> witzig <u>und</u> er ist immer hilfsbereit <u>oder</u> mitfühlend, er ist <u>aber</u> nie neidisch, <u>denn</u> er ist selbstsicher.

My best friend is not moody <u>but</u> witty <u>and</u> he's always helpful <u>or</u> sympathetic, <u>but</u> he's never jealous <u>because</u> he's confident.

SUBORDINATING CONJUNCTIONS

Although these conjunctions also help you to lengthen lists and sentences, they have a sting in their tail: like submarines they propel the verb to the end/bottom of the clause/sentence. Look what happens to these two sentences when you join them with <u>weil</u> (because):

Meine beste Freundin ist selbstsicher. Sie ist sehr intelligent und fleißig.
My best friend is confident. She is very intelligent.

Meine beste Freundin ist selbstsicher, <u>weil</u> sie sehr intelligent und fleißig <u>ist</u>.
My best friend is confident <u>because</u> she is very intelligent and hard working.

Here's the whole fleet:

als	when (in the past)	damit	so that	während	while/whilst
		dass	that	weil	because
bevor	before	ob	whether	wenn	if,
bis	until	obwohl	although		when(ever)

Because the verb has been sent to the bottom of the sentence by a sub(ordinating conjunction), it always stays at the bottom, even if it meets up with other words, such as separable verbs and infinitives.

SEPARABLE VERBS:
aussehen (to look)
With normal word order you get this:
Meine Schwester <u>sieht</u> sportlich <u>aus</u>.
My sister looks sporty.

But with <u>obwohl</u>, for example, the verbs sinks past <u>aus</u> and joins up with it:
Meine Schwester ist faul, <u>obwohl</u> sie sportlich <u>aussieht</u>.
My sister is lazy, <u>although</u> she looks sporty.

INFINITIVES:
kritisieren (to criticise)
Used as an infinitive, it normally looks like this:
Musst du ihn <u>kritisieren</u>?
Do you have to criticise him?

But add a sub(ordinating conjunction) like <u>ob</u> and the verb goes straight to the bottom/end:
Ich frage dich, <u>ob</u> du ihn kritisieren <u>musst</u>.
I'm asking you whether you have to criticise him.

Last but not least, if you really want to show how much you know about word order and subordinating conjunctions, remember that a whole subordinate clause can start a sentence but <u>it must be followed immediately by the main verb</u> (which is always the second idea/part of any sentence, like <u>ist</u> in this example, giving you two verbs together):

sub-verb	main verb

<u>Obwohl</u> sie sehr sportlich <u>aussieht</u>, <u>ist</u> meine Schwester ganz faul und überhaupt nicht fit.
<u>Although</u> she looks very sporty my sister <u>is</u> quite lazy and not at all fit.

ADJECTIVES

Whether you're Grumpy or Happy, Bashful or Dopey, Sleepy or Sneezy, a good dose of adjectives is what Doc orders.

- Wie ist dein (bester) Freund/Bruder/Vater?
  What is your (best) friend/brother/father like?

- Und deine (beste) Freundin/Schwester/Mutter?
  And your (best) (female) friend/sister/mother?

- Kannst du ihn/sie/sie beschreiben?
  Can you describe him/her/them?

POSITIV

bescheiden (modest)
fleißig (hard working)
freundlich (friendly)
höflich (polite)
intelligent (intelligent)
interessant (interesting)
klug (clever)
nett (nice)
witzig (funny, witty)

NEGATIV

angeberisch (boastful)
faul (lazy)
unfreundlich (unfriendly)
frech (rude)
dumm (stupid)
langweilig (boring)
doof (dopey, daft)
gemein (mean)
humorlos (humourless, unfunny)

When you use adjectives after their nouns, there is no need to change the endings:
Er/sie ist nett
He/she is nice
Wir/sie sind freundlich
We/they are friendly

But as soon as they come before the noun, their endings change to match the noun:
Masculine:
Nominative – Er ist ein netter Mensch
(He's a nice person)
Accusative – Ich habe einen netten Bruder
(I've got a nice brother)

Feminine:
Sie ist eine nette Frau (She's a nice woman)
Ich habe eine nette Schwester (I've got a nice sister)

Neuter:
Nominative – Das ist ein intelligentes Mädchen
(She's an intelligent girl)
Accusative – Ich suche ein intelligentes Mädchen
(I'm looking for an intelligent girl)

Do you know the endings when the adjectives follow 'der, die, das' and 'den, die, das'? Check on them!

IT'S ALL RELATIVE

Wie findest du deinen Bruder/deine Schwester?
What do you think of your brother/sister?

Ich finde ihn/sie toll.
I think he's/she's great.

Wie kommst du mit deinen Freunden/Eltern aus?
How do you get on with your friends/parents?

Ich komme mit ihnen gut/schlecht aus
I get on well/badly with them.

Wir verstehen uns gut.
We get on well together.

Ich habe ein enges Verhältnis zu meiner Oma.
I have a close relationship with my Grandma.

Meine Eltern verstehen mich nicht.
My parents don't understand me.

Bei uns gibt es immer Streit.
We're always arguing in our house.

Ich habe Probleme mit meinem Freund/mit der Schule/mit Geld.
I've got problems with my boyfriend/with school/with money.

Meine Familie/Alles nervt mich.
My family/Everything gets on my nerves.

Ich bin immer gleich sauer.
I'm always in a bad mood.

Ich habe alles satt!
I'm sick of everything!

Meine Freundin hat einen anderen.
My girlfriend has got another boyfriend.

MECKERECKE

WIE SIND EURE FREUNDE? UND EURE ELTERN?

Willkommen zu meiner 'Meckerecke'! Ich lade alle Jugendlichen ein, über ihre Freunde an mich zu schreiben. Lasst mal von Euch hören! Hoffentlich sind sie nicht wie die sieben Zwerge: mürrisch oder scheu, schläfrig oder.... Und eure Eltern? Wie kommt ihr mit ihnen aus? Schreibt bald wieder!
Jutta

Welcome to my 'Moaners' Corner! I invite all teenagers to write to me about their friends. Let's hear what you have to say! Let's hope they're not like the seven dwarfs: grumpy or bashful, sleepy or.... And what about your parents? How do you get on with them? Write back to me soon!
Jutta

MEINE FREUNDE SIND COOL ...

Liebe Jutta,
Ich kann ganz ehrlich sagen, dass ich gar keine Probleme mit meinen Freunden habe. Die meisten sind echt cool und wir verstehen uns prima! Meine beste Freundin Nadia ist so witzig, dass sie uns alle zum Lachen bringt, sobald sie die Rede hält. Eingebildet oder angeberisch ist sie aber nicht und wir streiten uns* selten. Sowas kann ich nicht leiden denn es nervt mich, wenn man meckert oder unglücklich ist. Niemand ist neidisch auf sie, obwohl sie einen netten festen Freund hat. Ich habe keinen festen Freund aber das ist mir egal, weil ich mit den meisten Jungen gut auskomme. Ich finde sie meistens treu und lieb und sie sind nie gemein zu mir. So ein Glück, echt tolle Freunde zu haben!
Susanne

Dear Jutta,
I can honestly say that I don't have any problems with my friends. Most of them are really cool and we get on great together! My best friend Nadia is so funny she makes us all laugh the moment she starts speaking. But she's not conceited or big headed and we hardly ever argue. I can't stand that sort of thing, when people moan or are unhappy. No one is jealous of her, even though she's got a steady boyfriend. I don't have a steady boyfriend but that doesn't bother me because I get on well with most of the lads. They're mainly loyal, nice friends and they're never mean to me. Aren't I the lucky one, to have such great friends!
Susanne

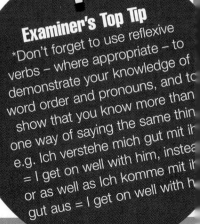

Examiner's Top Tip
*Don't forget to use reflexive verbs – where appropriate – to demonstrate your knowledge of word order and pronouns, and to show that you know more than one way of saying the same thing e.g. Ich verstehe mich gut mit ihm = I get on well with him, instead or as well as Ich komme mit ihm gut aus = I get on well with him.

MECKERECKE

MEINE ELTERN ABER ...

Liebe Jutta,
Bei uns gibt es immer Krach. Ich streite mich* fast jeden Tag mit meiner Mutter, und mein Vater versteht mich nicht. Warum? Weil sie zu viel von mir verlangen! Meine Mutter findet, dass ich nicht genug im Haushalt helfe, mein Bruder aber macht nichts. Warum kritisieren sie ihn denn gar nicht? Weil er jünger als ich ist, und weil er so fleißig in der Schule ist. Ich auch tue mein Bestes in der Schule, auch wenn ich schlechte Noten kriege. Wenn ich am Wochenende mit meinen Freunden ausgehen will, darf ich nicht später als zehn Uhr in der Disko bleiben, obwohl die Freunde bis Mitternacht dort bleiben dürfen. Was bin ich denn – Kind oder Erwachsener?! Bitte, Jutta, können Sie mir gute Ratschläge geben? Eltern verstehe ich gar nicht!
Philip

Dear Jutta
There are always rows in our house. I argue with my mother nearly every day and my father doesn't understand me. Why? Because they expect too much of me! My mother thinks I don't help with the housework enough, but my brother does nothing. So why don't they criticise him at all? Because he's younger than I am and because he works so hard at school. I try my best at school, too, even though I still get bad grades. If I want to go out at the weekend with my friends, I'm not allowed to stay later than ten o'clock at the disco, even though my friends can stay until midnight. Tell me, what am I – a child or an adult?! Please, Jutta, can you offer me any good advice? I don't understand parents at all!
Philip

CHARACTER AND PERSONAL RELATIONSHIPS ②

QUICK TEST

Say/write it in English:

1. Er ist bescheiden und fleißig.

2. Wie findest du deine Eltern?

3. Du bist nicht angeberisch oder eingebildet.

4. Frag ihn, ob er zur Party geht.

Say/write it in German:

5. Are they helpful?

6. I'm looking for a sympathetic (steady) boyfriend.

7. It's great that you get on well with them.

8. I have a close relationship with my mother.

9. We never argue, because that gets on my nerves.

10. We get on badly because he's mean to me.

THE CONDITIONAL

Q: WHY IS IT CALLED THE CONDITIONAL?
A: 'Simple – it won't happen unless certain
<u>conditions</u> are met:

Was <u>würdest</u> du machen, um die Umwelt zu schützen?
<u>Ich würde</u> so viel wie möglich recyceln.
What <u>would you do</u> to protect the environment?
<u>I'd</u> recycle as much as possible.

**Q: WHAT KEY WORD HELPS YOU TO
SPOT THE CONDITIONAL?**
A: 'Would':

Ich <u>würde</u> gefährdete Tierarten schützen.
Ich <u>möchte</u>* nicht schöne Tiere aussterben lassen.
<u>I'd/I would</u> protect endangered species.
I <u>wouldn't</u> like to let beautiful animals become
extinct

Q: HOW DO YOU FORM IT?
A: Simple – choose the part of 'würden' you need, to
say 'would', and add an infinitive at the end of the
sentence, where it usually goes:

'würden'		infinitive
ich würde (I would)	wir würden (we would)	recyceln (recycle)
du würdest (you would)	ihr würdet you (plural) would	schützen (protect)
er/sie/es/man würde (he/she/it/one would)	sie würden (they would)	benutzen (use)
Sie würden (you (singular & plural) would)		verschmutzen (pollute)

You do not need to use an infinitive with the verbs 'sein' to be** and 'haben' to have** to
form the conditional. Instead you simply choose the part you need from the grids below:

ich wäre	I would be	ich hätte	I would have
du wärst	you would be	du hättest	you would have
er sie es man } wäre	he she it would be one, etc	er sie es man } hätte	he she it would have one, etc
wir wären	we would be	wir hätten	we would have
ihr wärt	you (pl) would be	ihr hättet	you (pl) would have
sie wären	they would be	sie hätten	they would have
Sie wären	you (sing & pl) would be	Sie hätten	you (sing & pl) would have

Das wäre ideal
Was hättest du am liebsten?

That would be ideal
What would you like to have most?

Examiner's Top Tip
* As well as using 'ich möchte', etc to say 'I'd like', you can use 'ich hätte gern': Ich hätte gern unverschmutzte Luft I'd like unpolluted air

Examiner's Top Tip
** If you really want to score heavily in the exam, produce a couple of these sentences: 'wenn' (if) + the conditional of 'sein' o 'haben', followed by another verb in the conditional: Wenn ich genug Geld hätte, würde i alle Tiere schützen If I had enough money I'd protec all animals Wenn wir nicht so doof wären, w wir erneubare Energie benutze If we weren't so stupid, we'd use renewable energy

OUR ENVIRONMENT

Wie kann man die Umwelt schützen?
How can we/one protect the environment
Man kann/könnte
We/one can/could
benutzen/heizen mit/recyceln/sparen
use/heat with/recycle/save

MASKULINUM (DER)		FEMININUM (DIE)		NEUTRUM (DAS)	
Abfall	rubbish	Gefahr	danger	Altpapier	recycled paper
öffentlicher	public	Dose	tin, can	Gas	gas
Personenverkehr	transport	Sonnenenergie	solar power	Öl	oil
Lärm	noise	Sammelstelle	collection point	Recycling	recycling
Verkehrsstau	traffic jam	Verpackung	packaging	Wasser	water

THE PASSIVE: CAN YOU SUFFER IT?

The word 'passive' is derived from the same word as 'patient' – in other words, somebody who is suffering. You use the passive to say what is being done, has been done or will be done to someone or something.

AVOIDING THE PASSIVE

Although the passive is a good way of avoiding blame, e.g. 'The river has been polluted' rather than 'I have polluted the river', it is sensible to know other, simpler ways of saying the same thing. The most obvious is man (one, someone, we, you, they).
So:

Der Fluss ist verschmutzt worden.
The river has been polluted.

could easily become:

Man hat den Fluss verschmutzt.
Someone has polluted the river.

ACTIVE OR PASSIVE?

So far, all the verbs you have learnt have been (in the) active (voice):

Ich rauche. Ich verschmutze die Luft.
I'm smoking. I'm polluting the air.

Du trinkst Alkohol? Du bedrohst deine Gesundheit.
You're drinking alcohol? You're threatening your health.

They are active because the subject of the sentence (e.g. 'ich', 'du') carries out the action in the verb. With the passive (voice) it's the other way round: the action is done to the subject:

Die Luft ist verschmutzt worden.
The air has been/become polluted.

Seltene Tierarten werden gefährdet.
Rare species are (being) threatened.

Examiner's Top Tip
*Revise the full present, imperfect, perfect, pluperfect and future tenses of werden, as well as the conditional, so that you can use the passive for any person and any time.

FORMING THE PASSIVE

Passives are simple to form, provided you know the verb werden – to be(come)*:

Tense	'to be(come)' werden	+	a past participle
Present	is be(com)ing wird	→	vergiftet (poisoned)
Imperfect	was be(com)ing wurde	→	getötet (killed)
Perfect	has been/become ist	→	verschmutzt worden** (polluted)
Pluperfect	had been/become war	→	gefährdet worden** (threatened)
Future	will be(come) wird	→	recycelt werden (recycled)
Conditional	would be(come) würde	→	geheizt werden (heated)

Examiner's Top Tip
**With tenses that use the past participle of werden, (i.e. geworden), you drop the prefix ge- leaving worden:
Nicht genug Wasser ist gespart worden.
Not enough water has been saved = perfect tense.
Die Fische waren vergiftet worden.
The fish had been poisoned = pluperfect tense.

ENVIRONMENT 1

IMPERSONAL VERBS: IF IT HELPS...

You may not realise it, but you already know some impersonal verbs:

Es gibt keine Recyclingcontainers
There aren't any recycling bins
Es regnet
It's raining
Es ist acht Uhr
It's eight o'clock

The subject is usually es (it) and never I, you, etc. These are impersonal verbs because they do not involve a person. Sometimes they are also followed by a clause beginning with wenn (if, when(ever)) or by an infinitive clause (zu + infinitive):
Es gilt nichts, wenn man erneubare Energie nicht benutzen will.
It's no use/worth nothing, if we refuse to use renewable energy.
Es lohnt sich, so viel wie möglich zu recyceln.
It's worthwhile recycling as much as possible.

OTHER TENSES
If you need to use them in the imperfect, the perfect or the future tenses, just change them like this:
Es lohnte sich, die Umwelt zu schützen.
It was worthwhile protecting the environment.

Es hat sich gelohnt, Altpapier zu benutzen.
It (has) proved worthwhile using recycled paper.

Es wird sich lohnen, mit erneubarer Energie zu heizen.
It will be worthwhile heating with renewable energy.

ENVIRONMENT ②

UMWELTSCHUTZ

Was könnten wir machen, um die Umwelt besser zu schützen?
What could we do to protect the environment better than we do now?

Meiner Meinung nach* könnte man viel mehr tun.
In my opinion we could do much more?

Was zum Beispiel?
What for example?

Erstens sollte man so viel wie möglich recyceln: Abfall, Aludosen, Zeitungen, Glasflaschen, Plastiktüten.
First we should recycle as much as possible: rubbish, aluminium cans, newspapers, glass bottles, plastic bags.

Ist das alles?
Is that all?

Aber nein, es wäre am besten, wenn wir öffentlichen Personenverkehr benutzen würden, oder wenn man zu Fuß gehen oder mit dem Rad fahren würde.
Oh no, it would be best if we used public transport or went on foot or by bike.

MEINER MEINUNG NACH

Es tut mir so leid*, dass so viele seltene Tierarten getötet werden.
It upsets me so much that so many rare species are being killed.

Es ist zum Verzweifeln*, dass schöne unschuldige Tiere wie Elefanten erschossen werden, und zwar bloß weil man ihr Elfenbein verkaufen will.
It's enough to make you despair that beautiful, innocent animals such as elephants are shot, just because people want to sell their ivory.

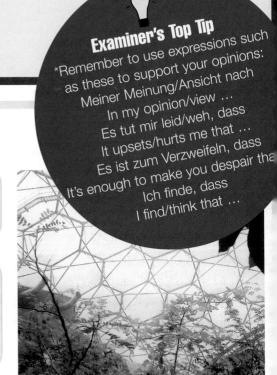

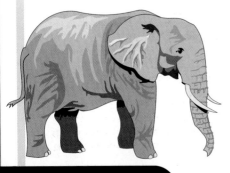

Es scheint nichts zu nützen, dass wir doch kein Elfenbein brauchen.
The fact that we don't actually need ivory doesn't seem to make any difference at all.

Wenn aber seltene Tierarten gefährdet sind, ist auch die Menschheit gefährdet.
However, if rare species are under threat, so is humanity.

DAS WÄRE IDEAL

Ich wohne in der Stadtmitte. Es gefällt mir gut, dass es hier so viel zu tun gibt, aber es gibt zu viel Lärm und zu viel Verkehr und alles wird verschmutzt. Wenn ich auf dem Land wohnen könnte, wäre das ideal. Aber nur wenn ich gleich in die Stadtmitte fahren könnte!

I live in the town centre. I'm pleased that there's so much to do here but there's too much noise and too much traffic and everything's getting polluted. If I lived in the country it would be ideal. But only if I could get into the town centre quickly!

Es wäre schön, wenn es keinen Treibhauseffekt, keinen Atommüll und keine Verschmutzung gäbe. Wir könnten dann alle schön ruhig zusammen leben. Wer würde es glauben?!

It would be lovely if there were no greenhouse effect, no nuclear waste and no pollution. Then we could all live together nice and peacefully. Who'd believe that?!

QUICK TEST

Say/write it in English:

1. Der Treibhauseffekt.

2. Man sollte alles recyceln.

3. Viele Tierarten werden gefährdet.

4. Es würde sich lohnen, öffentlichen Personenverkehr zu benutzen.

Say/write it in German:

5. One (= Man) should protect the environment.

6. Where would you like to live?

7. In my opinion there's too much noise.

8. We could use renewable energy.

9. What would they do if they had lots of money?

10. So many fish have been poisoned – it's enough to make you despair!

1. The greenhouse effect.
2. One/we should recycle everything.
3. Lots of species are under threat.
4. It would be worthwhile using public transport.
5. Man sollte die Umwelt schützen.
6. Wo möchtest du/möchten Sie wohnen/leben?
7. Meiner Ansicht/Meinung nach gibt es zu viel Lärm.
8. Wir könnten erneubare Energie benutzen.
9. Was würden sie machen, wenn sie viel Geld hätten?
10. So viele Fische sind vergiftet worden – es ist zum Verzweifeln!

EDUCATION, CAREERS AND FUTURE PLANS ❶

THE FUTURE TENSE

USING THE PRESENT TENSE FOR THE NEAR FUTURE

You can use the present tense to talk about things you will be doing shortly, as you can in English:

Nächste Woche fahren wir in Urlaub.

Next week we're going (= will be going) on holiday.

This use of the present instead of the future is very common in German and, as you saw on page 27, you can even use it to talk about future plans:

Ich verlasse die Schule und suche einen Job.

I'm going to leave/I'll leave school and (I'm going to/ I'll) look for a job.

USING 'WERDEN' + INFINITIVE TO FORM THE FUTURE TENSE

To talk about longer-term plans – and to impress examiners with your knowledge of tenses – simply use the present tense of <u>werden</u> and make sure the infinitive (the second verb, the one which tells you what you <u>will</u> <u>be</u> <u>doing</u>) goes to the end, like modal verbs.*

werden		infinitive	
ich	werde	I will/shall	<u>weiterstudieren</u> (continue studying)
du	wirst	you will	<u>reisen</u> (travel)
er/sie/es/man	wird	he/she/it/one	(einen Job) <u>suchen</u> (look for) (a job)
wir	werden	we will/shall	(Geld) <u>verdienen</u> (earn) (some money)
ihr	werdet	you will	(auf die Uni) <u>gehen</u> (go) (to university)
sie	werden	they will	(in einem Büro) <u>arbeiten</u> (work) (in an office)
Sie	werden	you will	(die Schule) <u>verlassen</u> (leave) (school)

<u>Test yourself</u>: using the grid above, you should be able to make at least ten more sentences in the future. Remember: you can use any of the infinitives with any of the parts of <u>werden</u>:

Hoffentlich** werden Sie einen Job suchen

Hopefully (I hope, we hope, etc) you'll look for a job.

EDUCATION, EDUCATION EDUCATION

- **Wenn ich meine Prüfungen bestehe, möchte ich/werde ich …**
  If I pass my exams I'd like to/ I'll …
  - **kurzfristig**
    short term
  - **langfristig**
    long term
  - **(mich) weiterqualifizieren**
    get (myself) further qualifications
  - **auf die Uni/Hochschule gehen**
    go to university

- **ein ganzes Jahr ohne Studium verbringen**
  spend a (whole) year away from studying
- **ins Ausland fahren**
  travel abroad
- **eine Weltreise machen**
  go round the world
- **(etwas) Geld verdienen**
  earn some money
- **meine Fremdspracherkenntnisse vertiefen**
  improve my foreign languages

- **Ich weiß noch nicht, was ich nächstes Jahr machen werde**
  I don't know what I'm going to do next year
- **es kommt darauf an**
  it depends

THE WORKING WORLD

Was werden Sie machen	What will you do?		
Was wollen Sie werden?	What do you want to become?		
Wie werden Sie Ihren Lebensunterhalt verdienen?	How will you earn your living?		

MASCULINE (DER)		FEMININE (DIE)		NEUTER (DAS)	
Beruf	occupation	Ausbildung	training	Marketing	marketing
Handel	business, commerce	Fernmeldetechnik	telecommunications		
Lehrling	apprentice	Hotellerie	hotel management, catering and hospitality		
Maschinenbau	engineering				
Tourismus	tourism	Informationstechnologie	ICT		

man muss kreativ sein	you must be creative
um einen solchen Beruf auszuüben	to do such an occupation
unabhängig	independent
logisch	logical
methodisch	methodical
original	original
praktisch	practical
verantwortlich	responsible

CAREERS AND JOBS

Arbeitsamt	Job Centre
Was würden Sie am liebsten machen/werden?	What would you most like to do/become?
Ich möchte ... werden	I'd like to be(come) a ...

Verkäufer	*Elektriker*	*Sekretär*
sales person	electrician	secretary
Verkäuferin	**Elektrikerin**	**Sekretärin**

Briefträger	*Bäcker*	*Fabrikarbeiter*
postman/-woman	baker	factory worker
Briefträgerin	**Bäckerin**	**Fabrikarbeiterin**

Bankangestellter	*Frisör*	*Krankenpfleger*
bank worker	hairdresser	nurse
Bankangestellte	**Friseuse**	**Krankenschwester**

Lehrer	*Arzt*	*Ingenieur*
Teacher	doctor	engineer
Lehrerin	**Ärtzin**	

THE YOUNG PERSON IN SOCIETY

ABITUR ODER JOB?

Haben Sie entschieden, was Sie nächstes Jahr machen werden?
Have you decided what you're going to do next year?
Nein, noch nicht, aber ich werde vielleicht versuchen, das Abitur zu machen.
No, not yet, but I'm going to try and do my A-Levels/Highers.
Sie werden also keinen Job suchen?
You're not going to look for a job?
Aber nein! Gar nicht! Das wäre so langweilig, finde ich. Zuerst sollte man auf die Uni gehen. Das ist viel interessanter.
No, definitely not. That would just be too boring, I think. You should go to university first. That's much more interesting....
... Danach kann man sich einen Beruf finden – mit Berufsausbildung, natürlich.
... Then you can find yourself a decent occupation – with professional training, of course.

ABITUR UND UNI

Welche Fächer werden Sie für das Abitur machen?
What A-Levels/Highers are you going to do?
Ich werde Mathe und Informatik insbesondere lernen, weil ich mich sehr für Informationstechnologie interessiere.
I'm very interested in ICT and computing, so in particular I'll be doing maths and computer studies.
Was passiert, wenn Sie das Abitur bestehen?
What happens if you pass your exams?
Dann werde ich an der Uni weiterstudieren. Und wenn nicht, wer weiß...?
I'll continue my studies at university. And if not, who knows...?

UND NACHHER?

Und nachher? Was für einen Beruf werden Sie wählen?
And after that? What occupation will you choose?
Tja, das ist ziemlich schwer zu sagen ... vielleicht Fernmeldetechnik.
Well, it's quite hard to say ... telecommunications, maybe.
Auf jeden Fall möchte ich meine Fertigkeiten verbessern und weitere Qualifikationen erhalten.
In any case, I'd like to upgrade my skills and get more qualifications.
Wollen Sie denn nicht Lehrer werden?
So, you don't want to be a teacher?
Doch, vielleicht. Wer weiß? Mal sehen.
Yes, perhaps. Who knows? We'll see

GRAMMAR CHECK

Re-read the texts and see how much you can remember:
The perfect tense: 'Haben Sie entschieden?'.
The present tense: 'das ist', 'ich interessiere mich', 'was passiert?'.
The future tense: 'ich werde versuchen', 'werden Sie wählen?'.
The conditional: 'Das wäre', 'man sollte'.
Modal verbs: 'sollte man', 'kann man', 'wollen Sie';

Subordinating: 'wenn Sie das Abitur bestehen?'
Conjunctions: 'weil ich mich sehr für Informationstechnologie interessiere'.
Adjectives: langweilig, interessanter, weitere.
Useful link words: 'also', 'aber', 'gar nicht', 'zuerst', 'danach', 'natürlich', 'und',
Expressions: 'insbesondere', 'dann', 'und nachher?', 'das ist ziemlich schwer zu sagen', Auf jeden Fall, 'doch, vielleicht'.
Put them all together and you're (almost) there!

EDUCATION, CAREERS AND FUTURE PLANS ②

BERUFSVORHERSAGE

- •Paul wird vielleicht Kaufmann werden, und zwar weil er gern reist …
  Paul will become a travelling salesman because he likes to travel …
  - •… und sich gern mit anderen Leuten trifft. Oder er wird vielleicht Lotse.
  … and meet people. Or perhaps he'll become a pilot.
    - •Es ist aber schwer, Lotse zu werden, darum wird er schwer arbeiten müssen, um seine Prüfungen zu bestehen. Er wird nicht heiraten.
  However, as it's difficult to become a pilot, he'll have to work hard and pass his exams. He won't get married.

- •Fatima wird sicherlich Tierärztin werden, weil sie alles gern hat, was mit …
  Fatima will definitely become a vet, because she likes everything to do with …
  - •… der Natur und Tieren zu tun hat. Es wird ihr gelingen, weil sie sehr intelligent ist. Sie wird heiraten und vier Kinder erzeugen.
  … nature and animals. She will succeed because she is intelligent. She'll get married and have four children.

- •Anke wird Lehrerin oder Grundschullehrerin werden. Und warum? Weil sie immer …
  Anke will become a secondary or primary school teacher. Why? Because she always …
  - •… guten Kontakt zu Kindern hat. Als Grundschullehrerin wird sie auch Mitglied …
  … gets on well with children. And, as a primary school teacher, she'll be a member …
    - •… einer beruflichen Mannschaft sein. Vielleicht wird sie ganz spät heiraten.
  … of a professional team. She might get married late in life.

- •Thomas wird vielleicht Taxifahrer werden … aber nein, das stimmt nicht, da er alleine arbeiten will.
  Thomas will be a taxi driver, perhaps … oh, no he won't, that's wrong, because he wants to work alone.
  - •Er wird sicherlich LKW Fahrer werdfen. Auf diese Weise wird er reisen können, ohne anderen Leuten begegnen zu müssen. Er wird dreimal heiraten und sich dreimal scheiden lassen.
  He'll definitely become an HGV driver. That way he'll be able to travel without having to meet other people. He'll get married and divorced three times.

QUICK TEST

Say/write it in English:

1. Du wirst die Schule verlassen.
2. Wir fahren am Wochenende in Urlaub.
3. Hoffentlich wird er nicht Frisör werden.
4. Werden sie genug Geld verdienen?

Say/write it in German:

5. She'll do A Levels.
6. I hope you find a job.
7. You ought to go to university.

8. What occupation will you choose?
9. Since he likes children he'll become a teacher.
10. If I don't pass my exams, I'll go round the world.

1. You'll leave school.
2. We're going on holiday at the weekend.
3. I (you/we, etc) hope/Hopefully he won't become a hairdresser.
4. Will they earn enough money?
5. Sie wird das Abitur machen.
6. Hoffentlich wirst du einen Job finden/findest du einen Job.
7. Man sollte auf die Uni gehen.
8. Was für einen Beruf werden Sie/wirst du/werdet ihr wählen?
9. Da er Kinder gern hat, wird er Lehrer (werden).
10. Wenn ich meine Prüfungen nicht bestehe, mache ich eine Weltreise/ werde ich eine Weltreise machen.

FAMILY AND SOCIAL PRESSURES

Was nervt Sie?
What gets on your nerves?

Was können Sie nicht leiden?
What can't you stand?

Leute, die* über nichts Anderes als Umweltprobleme oder Politik reden.
People who talk about nothing but environmental problems or politics.

Sogenannte Erwachsene, die uns immer wie Kinder behandeln.
So-called grown ups who always treat us like children.

Jugendliche, die keinen Spaß verstehen und nie Witze erzählen.
Young people who have got no sense of fun and who never tell jokes.

Leute, die alles ernst nehmen.
People who take everything seriously.

Lehrer, die nur für die Schule leben.
Teachers who only live for school.

Erwachsene, die glauben, wir können die Welt einfach verbessern.
Adults who think we can simply improve the world.

Es geht mir auf die Nerven, dass** meine Eltern mich nie ernst nehmen.
The fact that that my parents never take me seriously gets on my nerves.

Meine Eltern meckern andauernd und lassen mich nie in Ruhe.
My parents are forever moaning and never leave me in peace.

Meine Mutter ist immer todernst.
My mother is always deadly serious.

Maskulinum (der)		Femininum (die)	
Alkohol	alcohol	Arbeitslosigkeit	unemployment
Drogensüchtige	drug addict	Droge (n)	drug(s)
Ernst	seriousness	Erlaubnis	permission
Krebs	cancer	Heuchelei	hypocrisy
Sarkasmus	sarcasm	Humorlosigkeit	lack of humour
Scheinheilige	hypocrite	Krankheit	illness, sickness
Streit	arguing	Intoleranz	intolerance
Spaß	fun	doppelte Moral	double standards
Stress	stress	Politik	politics
Tabak	tobacco	Süchtigkeit	dependency
Witz	joke		

Examiner's Top Tip

*Remember you can score heavily by using relative pronouns who, that: der, die, das, etc., showing that you know that they send the verb to the end:
Ich kann Leute nicht leiden, die andauernd über Jugendliche meckern.
I can't stand people who are always moaning about young people.
**Equally, by using subordinating conjunctions, such as dass, weil and wenn, you can also boost your marks, again through your knowledge of word order:
Es ärgert mich, dass man mich nie ernst nimmt.
It makes me angry that people never take me seriously.

SOCIAL ILLS

Es gibt so viele Probleme für die Jugend von heute.
There are so many problems for the youth of today.

Am schlimmsten sind die Arbeitslosigkeit und die Unsicherheit.
Unemployment and uncertainty are the worst.

Ich habe Angst vor einem Atomkrieg.
I'm frightened of a nuclear war.

Für mich ist der Terrorismus das Schlimmste.
Terrorism is the worst thing in my view.

Meiner Meinung nach sind die lebensgefährlichen Krankheiten wie AIDS und Krebs das größte Problem.
In my opinion life-threatening illnesses such as AIDS and cancer are the greatest problem.

Die Drogensüchtigkeit ist ein großes Problem, aber das betrifft mich nicht.
Drug addiction is a big problem, but it doesn't affect me.

Doch, es geht uns alle an.
Yes it does, it concerns all of us.

PEER AND MEDIA PRESSURE

Es ist alles mit Image zu tun.
It's all to do with image.

Alle Mädchen sollen schlank und schön sein.
All girls are supposed to be slim and beautiful.

Persönlichkeit hat damit nichts zu tun.
Personality has got nothing to do with it.

Alle Jungen sollen cool sein.
All boys are supposed to be cool.

Wenn man sich nicht modisch ankleidet, ist man völlig aus.
If you don't follow the fashion you're definitely an outsider.

Wenn** man die ganze Werbung glaubt, ist das Aussehen am wichtigsten.
If we're to believe all the advertising, appearance is the most important thing.

Für mich ist das alles Blödsinn!
As far as I'm concerned, it's all a load of nonsense!

Alles, was Mode und Image betrifft, ist lauter Quatsch!
Everything to do with fashion and image is pure rubbish!

Klamotten sind auch so teuer! Die kann ich mir nicht kaufen.
Clothes are so expensive! I can't afford them.

Was sollte man machen, wenn man überhaupt nicht schlank und cool ist?
What are you supposed to do if you're not at all slim and cool?

Was soll ich machen, wenn alle meine Freunde auf Marken achten?
What am I supposed to do if my friends are all label freaks?

Das ist mir alles egal.
I don't care about any of it.

Image ist unwichtig – es hat nichts mit der Wirklichkeit zu tun.
Image is not important – it has nothing to do with reality.

Examiner's Top Tip
Notice again how useful modal verbs can be: here you have a chance to talk about what is supposed to happen and what people can and cannot afford.

SOCIAL ISSUES 1

Now that you've covered all the grammar and have learned lots of ways of expressing your opinions, giving reasons, writing and talking about a wide range of topics, you can tackle social issues and really make progress with your German. A lot of the language here will help you to impress in discussions with native speakers of German and will definitely give you a head start if you decide to continue studying German at a higher level.

AVOIDING PERSONAL PROBLEMS

Wie kann man ...
fit bleiben?
die Gesundheit bewahren?
guter Mitbürger sein?

How can you ...
stay fit?
keep healthy?
be a good citizen?

Man kann/muss ...
sich regelmässig üben
gesund essen und trinken
früh ins Bett gehen und früh aufstehen
Alkohol/Stress/Droge/Tabak/schlechte
Gewohnheiten vermeiden

You can/must ...
exercise regularly
eat and drink healthily
go to bed early and get up early
avoid alcohol/stress/drugs/
tobacco/bad habits

WAS ERWACHSENE VON UNS ERWARTEN

Wir haben unsere Leser gefragt: 'Was erwarten Erwachsene von euch?'

We asked our readers: 'What do adults expect of you?'

Ganz Gehrl ich gesagt*, erwarten alle Erwachsene zu viel von uns.

Das geht mir auf die Nerven, weil es laute Heuchelei ist.

Wir sollen schwer arbeiten, nie streiten, immer im Haushalt helfen.

Wir dürfen nicht lange in der Disco bleiben und sollen nette Freunde haben.

Was schlechte Gewohnheiten betrifft*, dürfen wir natürlich keinen Alkohol trinken. Tabak und Drogen sind auch untersagt. Nach der Schule werden wir selbstverständlich an der Uni studieren oder mindestens einen guten Job kriegen.

Auch wenn es Millionen von Arbeitslosen gibt. Angst vor Atomkrieg, Terrorismus, lebensgefährlichen Krankheiten und Umweltzerstörung kommt auch nicht in Frage: dafür sind wir zu jung.

Dazu habe ich nur eines zu sagen: wenn sie uns wie Kinder behandeln wollen, sollten sie nicht erstaunen, wenn wir uns genau wie Kinder und gar nicht wie Erwachsene benehmen.

Quite honestly, all adults expect too much of us.

It gets on my nerves because it's pure hypocrisy.

We're supposed to work hard, never argue, always help with the housework. We're not allowed to stay long at the disco and we're supposed to have nice friends.

As for bad habits, of course we're not allowed to drink alcohol. Tobacco and drugs are also banned. After school, it goes without saying that we'll go to university or get a good job. Even if there are millions of people unemployed. There's no question of us being afraid of nuclear war, terrorism, life-threatening diseases and the destruction of the environment: we're far too young for that. I've got just one thing to say to all that: if they want to treat us like kids, they shouldn't be surprised if we behave exactly like kids and nothing like adults.

LIEBER NICHT ERWACHSENER SEIN

Ich will eigentlich kein Erwachsener sein. Warum denn nicht? Ich komme doch gut mit meinen Eltern aus. Sie sind immer heiter und erzählen oft Witze. Auch meine Freunde finden sie ganz lieb. Das hat alles eigentlich mit ihnen nichts zu tun. Wie kann man seine Kinder nicht nur vor Teenagerproblemen sondern auch vor globalen Problemen wie Arbeitslosigkeit, Atomkrieg und Terrorismus schützen? Es ist nicht zum Erstaunen, dass es so viele Alkoholiker, Drogensüchtige und unglückliche Leute auf der Welt gibt. So schlecht ist die Kinderheit eigentlich nicht!

I don't really want to become an adult. Why not? I get on well with my parents. They're always cheerful and often crack jokes. My friends think they're nice, too. In fact it's got nothing to do with them. How can anyone protect their children not only from teenagers' problems but also from world issues such as unemployment, nuclear war and terrorism? It's not surprising there are so many alcoholics, drug addicts and unhappy people in the world. Childhood's not so bad after all!

HOFFENTLICH

Wir möchten Spaß haben, ohne das Leben die ganze Zeit zu ernst nehmen zu müssen. Wir möchten unsere Probleme womöglich alleine lösen, und wenn sie zu schwer alleine zu lösen sind, möchten wir sie ganz ruhig mit Eltern besprechen. Das heißt ohne Druck, ohne Stress und ohne Vorurteile! Wir wollen fit, gesund und glücklich sein. Wir wollen doch keine Top-Modelle sein und interessieren uns überhaupt nicht für Image, Geld und Werbung. Wir wollen nicht nationalistisch sein, wir sind lieber internationale Leute. Wir wollen keinen Alkohol und keine Droge. Hoffentlich werden wir Probleme wie die Arbeitslosigkeit und Intoleranz zusammen lösen.

We'd like to have fun without having to take life too seriously. We'd like to solve our problems on our own as far as possible and if they're too difficult to solve on our own we'd like to discuss them calmly with parents. That means without pressure, without stress and without pre-judging! We want to be fit, healthy and happy. We don't want to be top models and we're not the slightest bit interested in image, money and advertising. We don't want to be nationalistic either, we're international people. We don't want any alcohol or drugs. We hope we can solve the problems of unemployment and intolerance together.

SOCIAL ISSUES ②

QUICK TEST

Say/write it in English:

1. Das nervt mich.

2. Er kann es nicht leiden.

3. Arbeitslosigkeit ist am schlimmsten.

4. Es ärgert uns, dass Sie uns nicht ernst nehmen.

Say/write it in German:

5. What can't you stand?

6. They are afraid of nuclear war.

7. Everything to do with image and advertising is pure rubbish!

8. There are too many life-threatening diseases.

9. Let's hope we can solve the problem.

10. It's not surprising there are so many unhappy families.

10. Es ist nicht zum Erstaunen, dass es so viele unglückliche Familien gibt.
9. Hoffentlich können wir das Problem lösen.
8. Es gibt zu viele lebensgefährliche Krankheiten.
7. Alles, was Image und Werbung betrifft, ist lauter Quatsch!
6. Sie haben Angst vor Atomkrieg.
5. Was kannst du/könnt ihr nicht leiden?
4. It annoys us/makes us angry that you don't take us seriously.
3. Unemployment is the worst (thing).
2. He can't stand it.
1. That gets on my nerves.

Speaking

Role Play 1
You are talking to a German friend about what can be done to ease environmental problems:
• Say people could recycle as much as possible.
  (1 mark)
• Say people could use public transport. (1 mark)
• Say it's worthwhile using renewable energy.
  (1 mark)
• Ask your friend what (s)he would do. (1 mark)
                                        (4 marks)

Role Play 2
You are discussing with a German friend what you'll do when you finish your exams:
• Say you'll go on holiday. (1 mark)
• Say you'd like to get more qualifications. (1 mark)
• Say you hope to do your A-Levels/Highers.
  (1 mark)
• Ask him/her what (s)he'll do. (1 mark)
                                        (4 marks)

General Conversation

1. Wie kommst du mit deinen Freunden aus? (1 mark)
2. Wie ist dein bester Freund/deine beste Freundin? (2 Details) (1 mark)
3. Wie oft streitest du dich mit ihm/ihr? (1 mark)
4. Was wirst du nächstes Jahr machen? (1 mark)
5. Welche Fächer wirst du wählen, wenn du das Abitur machst? (1 mark)
6. Was für einen Beruf möchtest du? (1 mark)
7. Was möchtest du nicht werden? Warum? (2 marks)
8. Was würdest du machen, wenn du viel Geld hättest? (1 mark)
9. Wie kann man die Umwelt schützen? (1 mark)
10. Welche Umweltprobleme gibt es in der Stadmitte? (1 mark)
11. Was ist zum Verzweifeln, was seltene Tiere betrifft? (1 mark)

(12 marks)

Writing

1. Design a poster to promote environmental issues.
   Schreib folgende Sätze auf Deutsch:
• We must not pollute the environment any more! (1 mark)
• Fish are being poisoned! (1 mark)
• We must use recycled paper! (1 mark)
• We'd like to protect rare species! (1 mark)
• Would you like to help? (1 mark)

(5 marks)

2. Use your imagination: write up to 90 words on your ideal job, using the questions/prompts to help you:
   Mein idealer Beruf
   Beantworte folgende Fragen auf Deutsch:
• Was für einen Beruf möchtest du nicht wählen? (3 marks)
• Welchen Beruf wirst du machen? (3 marks)
• Warum denn? Wie arbeitest du am besten? Alleine? Als Mitglied in einer Mannschaft? In einem Büro? Draussen? (3 marks)
• Würdest du lieber reisen oder in einer Fabrik arbeiten? (3 marks)
• Wie muss man sein, um einen solchen Beruf auszuüben? (2–3 details) (3 marks)

(15 marks)

Reading

1. Lies folgenden Artikel.

Arbeit oder Erziehung?

Heutzutage finden die meisten Jugendlichen, dass es sich gar nicht lohnt, mit der Erziehung weiterzumachen. Sie meinen, die Schule und die Uni haben nichts mit der wahren Welt zu tun. Im Gegenteil haben Schulen und Universitäten etwas Unwirkliches an sich. Warum noch vier bis fünf Jahre weiterstudieren, wenn man sofort nach den Prüfungen seinen Beruf beginnen kann? Sonst wird man auch neidisch auf Freunde sein, die schon ihren Lebensunterhalt verdienen. Das ist nichts für die heutige Jugend.

Schreib R (Richtig) oder F (Falsch):
• Viele Jugendliche wollen lieber arbeiten als weiterstudieren.
• Die meisten glauben, dass es sich lohnt, auf die Hochschule zu gehen.
• Am liebsten werden sie mindestens vier Jahre arbeiten, bevor sie weiterstudieren.
• Am besten werden sie einen Job machen, um Geld sofort zu verdienen.
• Sie sind neidisch auf Studenten.

(5 marks)

2. Lies folgenden Text.

Meckerecke

Hoffentlich bin ich nicht die Einzige,⎡1⎤ Probleme ⎡2⎤ Hause hat. Bei uns ⎡3⎤ es andauernd Streit, und zwar weil meine Eltern mich kaum ⎡4⎤ . Vielleicht haben sie den ganzen ⎡5⎤ der Schule vergessen, ⎡6⎤ sie behaupten, ⎡7⎤ ich nie genug Hausaufgaben habe. Sie finden auch, dass mein Bruder fleissiger ⎡8⎤ ich ist, ⎡9⎤ sie überhaupt nicht so viel von ihm verlangen. Ich tue mein Bestes im Unterricht, auch ⎡10⎤ ich schlechte Noten bekomme. Das ist so unfair!

Schreib die passenden Buchstaben.
Beispiel: 1.D

A denn
B zu
C dass
D die
E wenn
F als

G gibt
H kritisieren
I obwohl
J hat
K verstehen
L Stress

(9 marks)

Eine bessere Welt?
Wie wäre es, wenn wir keine Umweltverschmutzung hätten? Wenn seltene Tiere nicht mehr gefährdet wären? Lohnt es sich nicht, schöne Tiere und Wälder, Seen und Flüsse zu schützen, so viel wie möglich zu recyceln, mit erneubarer Energie zu heizen, öffentlichen Personenverkehr zu benutzen? Wie lange noch müssen wir diese Situation leiden? Die Lösung ist doch klar. Sind wir aber bereit, die Verantwortung anzunehmen?

3. Lies folgenden Text:
Beantworte folgende Fragen auf Deutsch:
a) Wie ist die Umwelt im Moment? (1 mark)
b) Was könnte man machen, um Fische nicht mehr zu vergiften? (2 marks)
c) Wie kann man Energie sparen? (2 Details) (3 marks)

(6 marks)

How did you do?

1–20	correct	start again
21–35	correct	getting there
36–49	correct	good work
50–60	correct	excellent

ANSWERS

My World

Speaking
Role Play 1
1. Was machst du nach der Schule? (1 mark)
2. Ich muss meine Hausaufgaben machen. (1 mark)
3. Kannst du/Können wir am Freitagabend ausgehen? (1 mark)
4. Wir können uns um acht Uhr in der Stadtmitte treffen. (1 mark)

(4 marks total)

Role Play 2
1. Ich fahre mit dem Bus/Auto/Rad zur Schule/Ich gehe zu Fuß zur Schule. (1 mark)
2. In der Mittagspause treffe ich mich mit meinen Freunden im Schulhof. Meistens esse ich Butterbrote, Chips und Obst und trinke eine Cola. (1 mark)
3. In der Schule haben wir einen Computerverein und eine Fußballmannschaft. (1 mark)
4. Musst du eine Schuluniform tragen? (1 mark)

(4 marks total)

General Conversation
1. Ja, ich habe einen Hund/eine Katze/ein Kaninchen/Nein, ich habe keine Haustiere. (1 mark)
2. Ich wohne mit meiner Mutter, meinem Vater und meinem Bruder. Mein Bruder heißt Liam. Er ist zehn Jahre alt und sehr sportlich. (1 mark)
3. Ich komme mit meinen Eltern sehr gut aus, aber meinen Bruder finde ich launisch und ein bisschen doof. (1 mark)
4. Mein Vater ist fleißig und freundlich. Er ist Kaufmann bei Kodak und kommt aus Schottland. Meine Mutter ist Kassiererin. Sie ist ziemlich klein und sie ist Engländerin. (1 mark)
5. Ich spiele Basketball und Tennis und im Winter fahre ich ski. Zu Hause lese ich und sehe fern. (1 mark)
6. Ich wohne in Portsmouth. Das ist eine große Stadt in Südengland, aber ich bin in Southampton geboren. (1 mark)
7. Mein Haus ist ziemlich alt und klein, mit sechs Zimmern. Im Erdgeschoss gibt es die Küche (etc.). Im ersten Stock haben wir drei Schlafzimmer.... Das Haus gefällt mir, weil es bequem und hübsch ist. (1 mark)
8. Ich habe mein eigenes Schlafzimmer, aber es ist ganz klein. Die Wände sind blau und der Teppich ist dunkelblau. Ich habe einen Schreibtisch mit meinem Computer. (1 mark)
9. Ich stehe normalerweise um sieben Uhr auf. Erstens dusche ich dann frühstücke ich. Meistens trinke ich Tee und esse Toast. Ich verlasse das Haus gegen Viertel vor acht (1 mark)
10. Ich besuche eine große Gesamtschule. Sie ist ziemlich modern. Wir haben ungefähr tausend Schüler und Schülerinnen. Es gibt eine Bibliothek, eine Turnhalle.... (1 mark)
11. Dieses Jahr lerne ich neun Fächer. Mein Lieblingsfach ist Deutsch, weil der Lehrer sympathisch ist. Ich finde Geschichte langweilig und ich mag Physik nicht, weil die Lehrerin zu streng ist. (1 mark)
12. Wir müssen alle Schuluniform tragen. Das finde ich doof. Sie ist hässlich und altmodisch. Man darf nicht in der Schule rauchen und Drogen sind verboten. Meiner Meinung nach ist das gut, weil sie gefährlich sind. (1 mark)

(12 marks total)
(Total for Speaking: 20 marks)

Writing
1. Bett/Kleiderschrank/Schreibtisch/Teppich/Fernseher (etc.)
(1 mark for each, based on spelling. 4 marks total)
(Marks based on spelling and grammatical accuracy)
2. •Dieses Jahr lerne ich neun Fächer: Englisch, Mathe.... (2 marks)
•Ich mag Französisch nicht ... (2 marks)
•... weil der Lehrer langweilig ist/weil es zu schwer ist.... (2 marks)
•Meistens sind meine Lehrer sehr nett, aber die Englischlehrerin finde ich zu streng. (2 marks)
•Wir haben sieben Stunden pro Tag. (2 marks)
•Nach der Schule kann man in den Informatikraum gehen und Internet surfen. Es gibt auch einen Theaterverein.... (2 marks)
•Meine Schuluniform ist schwarz und ziemlich modern. Jungen und Mädchen müssen ein schwarzes Sweatshirt und eine schwarze Hose tragen. Mädchen dürfen auch ein Kleid tragen. (2 marks)
•Wie ist deine Schule?/Was ist dein Lieblingsfach?/Wann beginnt der Unterricht? (2 marks)
(16 marks total)
(Total for Writing: 20 marks)

Reading
1. a) Budgie/budgerigar. (1 mark)
b) Piano. (1 mark)
c). (Any 2 of) New/Five rooms/In the town centre. (2 marks)
d). (Any 1 of) Wardrobe/Desk/Carpet. (1 mark)

(5 marks total)

2. 2F 3H 4C 5G 6D 7A 8E
(1 mark each)

(7 marks total)

3. 2J 3I 4K 5B 6C 7E 8D 9F
(1 mark each)

(8 marks total)
(Total for Reading: 20 marks)
(Test Total: 60 marks)

Holiday Time and Travel 1

Speaking
Role Play 1
1. (Bus)Linie fünfundfünfzig. (1 mark)
2. Steigen Sie am Bahnhof aus. (1 mark)
3. Das Schloss ist hinter dem Dom. (1 mark)
4. Sie fahren alle zehn Minuten. (1 mark)

(4 marks total)

Role Play 2
1. Haben Sie noch Zimmer frei? (1 mark)
2. Ich möchte ein Familienzimmer für fünf Nächte. (1 mark)
3. (Ich möchte) ein Zimmer mit Dusche. (1 mark)
4. Ist das mit Frühstück? (1 mark)

(4 marks total)

General Conversation
1. Am liebsten mache ich einen Sporturlaub, etc. (1 mark)
2. Weil ich sehr gern Sport treibe, etc. (1 mark)
3. Ich fahre nach Spanien, etc./Ich bleibe zu Hause. (1 mark)
4. Meistens fahre ich nach Deutschland, etc. (1 mark)
5. In den Sommerferien/Am Ende Juli/Am Anfang August, etc. (1 mark)
6. Normalerweise für vierzehn Tage, etc. (1 mark)
7. Ich fliege mit meinen Eltern, etc. (1 mark)
8. Ich faulenze/sonne mich/mache Ausflüge, etc. (1 mark)
9. Es gibt Kirchen/historische Gebäude/Museen/etc. (1 mark)
10. Es gibt nicht viel für Jugendliche, etc. (1 mark)
11. Meistens ist das Wetter schön, etc. (1 mark)
12. Es gibt das Stadion, Cafés, etc. (1 mark)

(12 marks total)
(Total for Speaking: 20 marks)

Writing
1. (2 marks per question based on spelling and grammatical accuracy)
•Ich möchte einen Platz/für zehn Tage im August reservieren. (2 marks)
•Wir sind drei Personen/und ein Auto und ein Wohnwagen. (2 marks)
•Gibt es ein Schwimmbad/auf dem Campingplatz? (2 marks)
•Namens Jones./Was kostet das (alles)? (2 marks)

(8 marks total)

2. (2 marks per question based on spelling and grammatical accuracy)
•Ich fahre lieber/im Winter in Urlaub, etc. (2 marks)
•Ich treibe gern Sport, etc./Ich fahre gern Ski, zum Beispiel, etc. (2 marks)
•Ich fahre lieber/mit meinen Freunden/alleine, etc. (2marks)
•Am liebsten laufe ich/ im Sommer Wasserski, etc. (2 marks)
•Dieses Jahr fahre ich/mit meinem Bruder nach Griechenland, etc. (2 marks)
•Und du? Wohin fährst du/dieses Jahr in Urlaub? (2 marks)
(12 marks total)
(Total for Writing: 20 marks)

Reading
1. 2G 3F 4C 5A
(4 marks)

2. 2I 3K 4J 5F 6A 7G 8B 9E
(8 marks)

3.. a) (das ist der) Winter. (1 mark)
b) Es sind bald Weihnachtsferien. (1 mark)
c) Man kann zum Hotel Alpenhorn fahren. (1 mark)
d) In den Alpen. (1 mark)
e) Die Schweiz ist in der Nähe. (1 mark)
f) Herr Schultz ist der Hoteldirektor. (1 mark)
g) Man kann schwimmen und Gymnastik/Aerobik, etc. machen. (2 marks)

(8 marks total)
(Total for Reading: 20 marks)
(Test Total: 60 marks)

Holiday Time and Travel 2

Speaking
Role Play 1
1. Ich habe einen Tisch für zwei Personen reserviert. (1 mark)
2. In der Ecke. Haben Sie die Speisekarte? (1 mark)
3. Hähnchen mit Pommes frites und grünen Bohnen. (1 mark)
4. Einen Orangensaft und ein Mineralwasser. (1 mark)

(4 marks total)

Role Play 2
1. Was kostet ein Brief nach England, bitte? (1 mark)
2. (Ich möchte) vier Briefmarken zu fünfundsiebzig Cents. (1 mark)
3. Ich möchte auch dieses Paket nach Spanien schicken. (1 mark)
4. Können Sie es wiegen, bitte? (1 mark)

(4 marks total)

General Conversation
1. Ich bin in die Stadt gegangen, etc. (1 mark)
2. Ich bin um halb neun aufgestanden. (1 mark)
3. Ich bin zu Hause geblieben, etc. (1 mark)
4. Mit meinem besten Freund, etc. (1 mark)
5. Wir hatten Fußball gespielt, etc. (1 mark)
6. Es war toll! (1 mark)
7. Ich habe sie/meine Sommerferien in Frankreich verbracht. (1 mark)
8. Ich bin mit meinen Eltern gefahren. (1 mark)
9. Wir sind drei Wochen dort geblieben. (1 mark)
10. Wir haben in einem Luxushotel am Strand gewohnt. (1 mark)
11. Es war fantastisch! etc. (1 mark)
12. Wir haben jede Menge Sehenswürdigkeiten besichtigt, etc. (1 mark)

(12 marks total)
(Total for Speaking: 20 marks)

Writing
1. (Based on spelling and grammatical accuracy):
•Ich habe meinen Koffer verloren. (1 mark)
•Ich habe ihn vielleicht im Flur verloren. (1 mark)
•Er ist braun/und er ist aus Leder. (2 marks)
•Drinnen waren/ mein Laptop und ein Fotoapparat. (2 marks)
•Der Laptop ist ziemlich klein und schwarz./Das ist ein Toshiba. (2 marks)

(8 marks total)

2. (Based on spelling and grammatical accuracy)
•Letzten Sommer bin ich nach Rom gefahren. (2 marks)

•Ich bin mit meinen Eltern, etc./
dorthin gefahren. (2 marks)
•(Nein) wir sind (von Heathrow,
etc.)/geflogen. (2 marks)
•(Ja) jede Menge Jugendliche habe
ich kennengelernt./Das war cool!
(2 marks)
•Am besten hat mir/die Stadtmitte
Rom gefallen. (2 marks)
•Und du? Bist du in Urlaub
gefahren?/Was hast du gemacht?
(2 marks)

(12 marks total)
(Total for Writing: 20 marks)

Reading
1. a) Stomach ache (1 mark)
b) Postcards (1 mark)
c) Lost property office (1 mark)
d) Dentist (1 mark)
e) Bureau de change/Money
changing office (1 mark)
(5 marks total)

2. 1F 2R 3F 4F 5R
(5 marks total)

3. a) Er war vor zwei Monaten /auf
Urlaub in Bayern. (2 marks)
b) Es hatte begonnen,/zu regnen. (Es
regnete/Es war regnerisch) (2 marks)
c) Weil die Straße/ nass war.
(2 marks)
d) Sie haben die Polizei/und die
Feuerwehr angerufen. (2 marks)
e) Der Polizist, der ihm Fragen
gestellt hat/hat es ihm gesagt.
(2 marks)

(10 marks total)
(Total for Reading: 20 marks)
(Test Total: 60 marks)

Work and Lifestyle

Speaking
Role Play 1
1. Ich möchte / hätte gern fünf
Hundert Gramm Pilze, bitte. (1 mark)
2. Haben Sie Erdbeeren, bitte?
(1 mark)
3. Ich nehme ein Kilo Birnen, bitte.
(1 mark)
4. Was kostet das, bitte? (1 mark)
(4 marks total)

Role Play 2
1. Ich suche/möchte eine Hose, bitte.
(1 mark)
2. Diese hier gefällt mir. (1 mark)
3. Darf ich sie bitte anprobieren?
(1 mark)
4. Sie ist mir zu groß. (1 mark)
(4 marks total)

General Conversation
1. Jede Woche räume ich mein
Zimmer auf/Abends decke ich den
Tisch/Ich spüle immer ab (1 mark)
2. Letztes Wochenende habe ich das
Auto gewaschen/habe ich
eingekauft/habe ich den Rasen
gemäht (1 mark)
3. Das ist verschieden. In der Woche
isst man oft kalt: Butterbrote oder
Salat. Aber am Wochende ist man
manchmal heiß, besonders am
Sonntag. Zum Beispiel isst man
Suppe, Hähnchen und Gemüse
(1 mark)
4. Heute habe ich Müsli und Toast
mit Marmelade gegessen und ein
Glas Apfelsaft getrunken. (1 mark)
5. Mein Lieblingsgericht ist Nudeln
mit Zwiebeln, Tomaten, Pilzen und
Käse. (1 mark)

6. Ja, ich esse meistens gesund: fast
nichts Fettiges und nicht viel Fleisch
– ich esse lieber Fisch. Ab und zu
esse ich Schokolade, aber normalerweise kaufe ich Obst oder Joghurt.
(1 mark)
7. Ich bin nicht sehr sportlich, aber
ich schwimme gern – mindestens
zweimal in der Woche. Ich rauche
nicht und trinke fast keinen Alkohol –
nur ein kleines Glas Wein zum
Abendessen. (1 mark)
8. Nein, ich habe keinen
Teilzeitjob./Ja, Samstags arbeite ich
an der Kasse, in einem Supermarkt.
Ich mache sechs Arbeitsstunden und
verdiene dazu dreißig Pfund pro Tag.
Damit kaufe ich Computerspiele und
spare für ein neues Rad. (1 mark)
9. Ich machte mein Arbeitspraktikum
in einem Büro. Ich half dem Chef
und musste Akten organisieren und
fotokopieren. Manchmal fand ich es
ziemlich langweilig aber die anderen
Leute waren ganz freundlich. (1 mark)
10. In dem Dorf wo ich wohne, gibt
es nichts. Man muss mit dem Bus in
die Stadt fahren – dort gibt es ein
Kino, ein Hallenbad und ein
Internetcafé. Man kann auch zum
Jugendklub gehen. Ich bin damit
nicht ganz zufrieden – es gibt nicht
viel für junge Leute. (1 mark)
11. Letzte Woche habe ich den Film
'Harry Potter' gesehen. Es handelt
sich um einen Jungen, der Zauberer
ist und viele Abendteuer hat, sobald
er eine Hexeschule besucht. Der Film
war ganz spannend und sehr
komisch. (1 mark)
12. Letzten Samstag habe ich mit
meinem/meiner besten
Freund/Freundin einen
Einkaufsbummel gemacht. Wir sind
ins Einkaufszentrum gegangen. Dort
gibt es allerlei Geschäfte. Zu Mittag
haben wir Pizza und Eis in einem
italienischen Restaurant gegessen.
Danach habe ich mir ein schönes T-
Shirt gekauft und mein(e) Freund(in)
hat eine CD von seiner/ihrer
Lieblingsgruppe gekauft. Nächsten
Samstag gehen wir in London
einkaufen. (1 mark)

(12 marks total)
(Total for Speaking: 20 marks)

Writing
•Ich bekomme zehn Pfund
Taschengeld pro Woche./Ich
bekomme kein Taschengeld. (1 mark)
•Ich habe keinen Teilzeitjob./Ich
arbeite in einem Supermarkt./Ich
trage Zeitungen aus./Ich bin
Babysitter(in)./Ich verdiene … Pfund
pro Monat./Ich kaufe …/Ich spare
mein Geld für … (1 mark)
•Mein Job gefällt mir gut, weil er gut
bezahlt ist/weil ich Kinder gern
habe./Mein Job gefällt mir nicht, weil
er langweilig ist … (1 mark)
•Ich machte mein Arbeitspraktikum bei
einer Firma/in einem Büro. (2 marks)
•Ich musste Kunden anrufen/Briefe
schreiben/fotokopieren. (2 marks)
•Es hat mir gut gefallen …/Es hat mir
nicht gefallen … (1 mark)
•…weil die Arbeit interessant
war/weil die anderen Leute freundlich waren./… weil ich es total
langweilig fand./weil die anderen
Leute nicht sehr nett waren. (1 mark)
•Was musst du in deinem Teilzeitjob
machen?/Wie viel Geld verdienst
du?/Was sind deine Arbeitsstunden?
(1 mark)

(10 marks total)

2. (Marks based on spelling and
grammatical accuracy)
•Das wichtigste Fest für mich/uns ist
Weihnachten/Hannukah/Ramadan/
Diwali … (1 mark)
•Ich habe dieses Fest sehr gern, weil
es viel Spaß macht/weil alle glücklich
sind … (2 marks)
•Man schenkt Geschenke/zündet
Kerzen an/singt/schickt Karten …
(1 mark)
•Der Tradition nach isst man
Truthahn und Plumpudding./Man isst
nichts während … Tage.(1 mark)
•Ich hatte am (achten Dezember)
Geburtstag. Am Wochenende bin ich
mit meiner Familie zu einem
Themenpark gefahren./Ich habe eine
Party gegeben./Ich habe meine
Freunde eingeladen. Es war toll!/Es
hat viel Spaß gemacht. (2 marks)
•Ich hatte ein neues Rad/eine
Armbanduhr/einen Computer von
meinem Vater/von meiner Mutter/von
meinen Eltern bekommen. (1 mark)
•Zum nächsten Geburtstag möchte
ich Disneyland Paris besuchen/eine
Party geben/ins Kino mit meinen
Freunden gehen/einen Fernseher
bekommen.
(2 marks)

(10 marks total)
(Total for Writing: 20 marks)

Reading
1. 1R 2F 3R 4F 5F
(5 marks)

2. 2J 3I 4A 5F 6B 7C 8G 9K
(8 marks)

3. a) Ja, er (sein Teilzeitberuf) gefiel
ihm (Dieter). (1 mark)
b) Weil er die Arbeit unterschiedlich
und interessant fand/Weil er Tiere
(so) gern hat/hatte. (1 mark)
c) Die Vögel aßen Obst (Äpfel,
Bananen, usw). (1 mark)
d) Er (Dieter) musste den
Meerschweinchen Gemüse geben.
(1 mark)
e) Ein (böses) Kaninchen hat ihn
verletzt/hat ihm die Hand gebissen.
(1 mark)
f) Er hatte Angst vor (den)
Schlangen. (1 mark)
g) Er (Dieter) möchte Tierarzt
werden. (1 mark)

(7 marks)
(Total for Reading: 20 marks)
(Test Total: 60 marks)

The Young Person in Society

Speaking
Role Play 1
1. Man könnte so viel wie möglich
recyceln. (1 mark)
2. Man könnte öffentlichen
Personenverkehr benutzen. (1 mark)
3. Es lohnt sich, erneuerbare Energie
zu benutzen. (1 mark)
4. Was würdest du machen? (1 mark)
(4 marks total)

Role Play 2
1. Ich fahre in Urlaub/Ich werde in
Urlaub fahren. (1 mark)
2. Ich möchte mich weiterqualifizieren. (1 mark)
3. Hoffentlich werde ich das Abitur
machen/mache ich das Abitur.
(1 mark)
4. Was wirst du machen? (1 mark)
(4 marks total)

General Conversation
1. Ich komme mit ihnen/mit meinen
Freunden gut aus. (1 mark)
2. Er/Sie ist witzig und hilfsbereit,
etc. (1 mark)
3. Ich streite mich oft/selten/nie mit
ihm/ihr. (1 mark)
4. Ich mache das Abitur/Ich suche
einen Job. (1 mark)
5. Ich werde Mathe, Physik und
Chemie, etc machen/wählen. (1 mark)
6. Ich möchte Ingenieur, etc werden.
(1 mark)
7. Ich möchte nicht Lehrer(in) werden, weil ich nicht mehr auf der
Schule bleiben will, etc. (2 marks)
8. Ich würde eine Weltreise machen,
etc. (1 mark)
9. Man kann Altpapier benutzen, alles
recyceln, etc. (1 mark)
10. Es gibt zu viel Lärm und zu viel
Verkehr, etc. (1 mark)
11. Sie werden gefährdet/getötet, etc.
(1 mark)

(12 marks total)
(Total for Speaking: 20 marks)

Writing
1. (based on spelling and grammatical
accuracy)
•Wir müssen/Man muss die Umwelt
nicht mehr verschmutzen! (1 mark)
•Fische werden vergiftet! (1 mark)
•Wir müssen/Man muss Altpapier
benutzen! (1 mark)
•Wir möchten seltene Tiere schützen!
(1 mark)
•Möchten Sie (mit)helfen? (1 mark)
(5 marks total)

2. Mein idealer Beruf
Ich möchte nicht
Lastkraftwagenfahrer/oder
Büroangestellter werden/und ich
möchte nicht in einer Fabrik arbeit-
en./Ich werde vielleicht Tierarzt werden,/denn ich arbeite gern mit
Tieren/und ich treffe mich auch gern
mit Leuten./Am besten arbeite ich
draussen/in der Natur/aber ich
möchte auch Mitglied in einer
Mannschaft sein,/die Tiere schützt
(heilt)./Ich würde besonders
gern reisen,/obwohl ich nie in einem
Büro arbeiten würde./Um Tierarzt zu
sein,/muss man unabhängig/und
mitfühlend sein.
(1 mark per section = 15 marks total)
(Total for Writing: 20 marks)

Reading
1. 1R 2F 3F 4R 5F
(5 marks)

2. 2B 3G 4K 5L 6A 7C 8F 9I 10E
(9 marks)

3. a) Die Umwelt/Sie ist verschmutzt.
(1 mark)
b) Man könnte die Seen/und Flüsse
schützen. (1 mark)
c) Man kann/mit erneuerbarer Energie
heizen/und öffentlichen
Personenverkehr benutzen.
(3 marks)
(Total for Reading: 20 marks)
(Test Total: 60 marks)

INDEX